SEXUAL HARASSMENT

IN THE WORKPLACE

HOW TO PREVENT, INVESTIGATE, AND RESOLVE PROBLEMS IN YOUR ORGANIZATION

ELLEN J. WAGNER

amacom

American Management Association

Library of Congress Cataloging-in-Publication Data

Wagner, Ellen J.
    Sexual harassment in the workplace : how to prevent, investigate,
and resolve problems in your organization / Ellen J. Wagner.
        p.   cm.
    Includes bibliographical references and index.
    ISBN 0-8144-7787-9
    1. Sexual harassment--Investigation.   I. Title.
HD6060.3.W34   1992
658.3'145--dc20   92-4324
                                                                  CIP

Printing number

10   9   8   7   6   5   4   3   2

For my
husband
with love and thanks.

Contents

Acknowledgments

I'd like to acknowledge the practical assistance and personal encouragement of Diane Dann and Linda Kline. Their friendship, and their help, made writing this book a lot easier.

SEXUAL HARASSMENT

IN THE WORKPLACE

1

First Considerations

During the last decade, sexual harassment has become a subject of increasing concern for large and small employers alike, as well as for all levels of employees, the media, and the public. During the fall 1991 Senate Judiciary Committee hearings on the sexual harassment allegations Professor Anita Hill lodged against Supreme Court nominee Clarence Thomas, Americans sat before their television screens transfixed, but not a little confused.

Over the course of the hearings, we slowly learned what employers have known for some time: that sexual harassment situations are fraught with pitfalls, that the truth can be elusive as claims and counterclaims compete for credibility. Employers have long faced the need to elicit details, attempt to verify them through corroborating witnesses and workplace documentation, assess the facts and credibility of those involved, and make decisions on how best to resolve the situation.

In the course of handling sexual harassment situations, employers have come to understand that this very sensitive area can be difficult to deal with, disruptive to the workplace, and disagreeable to all concerned. And the stakes are high and getting higher. In an increasingly litigious society and in an era of ever-increasing employee rights and employer responsibilities, sexual harassment allegations are particularly hazardous. Everyone involved has rights, and frequently these rights conflict.

Employers face the possibility both of administrative action through government oversight agencies and of civil suits where common-law negligence claims can result in extensive punitive damages. Corporate officials, managers, and human resources professionals may face the possibility of personal liability for their actions in dealing with harassment situations, or for their failure to deal with them effectively. Charging parties and other employees may face personal liability for spreading unproven allegations, gossip, and innuendo in the workplace or in the community at large.

Yet employers have a duty to provide a workplace free of harassment and unwelcome sexual advances. In order to do that, employers must navigate the minefield of rights and obligations and attempt to uncover the truth, end any illegal conduct, and restore harmony to the workplace.

It has long been a truism that sexual harassment complaints represent a minuscule percentage of actual harassment situations. The reasons for this "tip of the iceberg" phenomenon are relatively easy to ascertain: embarrassment, self-blame, and fear of what will happen professionally and personally if complaints are lodged.

When these feelings affect the employee's performance at work, the productivity, focus, and effectiveness of the individual and the group may suffer as the victim of harassment attempts to cope with her situation and coworkers wonder what the company will do to end the harassing behavior, when and how it will act. The frequency of constructive discharge (when an employee is not fired, but feels forced to resign) related to sexual harassment activity, the increase in turnover, and related expenses incurred in training replacement employees are all hidden costs of harassment in a workplace where nonmanagerial workers are still overwhelmingly women.

Although harassers and harassees come in both sexes, the great majority of situations involve one or more male harassers and a lower-level female harassee. *She* is therefore still very much a proper pronoun when sexual harassment is discussed, and this book uses these most common genders for ease of identification throughout.

While sexual harassment is clearly a pervasive reality, every case needs to be reviewed on its own merit. Just because harassment is a significant social and corporate problem does not mean it has in fact occurred in a particular instance. Equally detrimental to an organization's overall health is the failure to safeguard the reputation of the accused from the gossip and innuendo that frequently form a central part of workplace social life. This is so even if an investigator finds that a sexual harassment allegation has some merit, and, of course, even more so when the finding is that harassment did not occur or the evidence is inconclusive.

Regardless of the finding, or the merits of the case, employers are well aware of today's realities and the ease with which any employee can sue on a variety of bases at any time, with or without real merit to the cause. At the least, employers must pay the costs of defending their organizations (and sometimes themselves) from frivolous claims just as they must from claims with real merit, devoting considerable time and effort to that end. In addition to damage to an organization's employee relations, even frivolous claims can directly affect an employer's public image, generating negative press and public relations or creating difficulties for the company in its community affairs, not to mention the possible impact of lower sales and/or lower productivity.

The employer's responsibilities in this area are serious and complex, easily able to overwhelm a conscientious line or staff person charged with carrying them out on the organization's behalf. This book aims to help clarify sexual harassment rights and responsibilities and to provide "how to" suggestions for dealing swiftly and effectively with sexual harassment, determining what happened, and responding with corporate actions appropriate to the facts. Perhaps even more important, this book also offers prevention strategies that employers can (and should) use to stop sexual harassment before it begins, minimizing the risks to the organization and the people working in it.

2

The Scope of the Problem

Over the last few years, as the anecdotal evidence of sexual harrassment has mounted, various attempts have been made to quantify the incidence of sexual harassment and learn more about who typically brings sexual harassment allegations to the agencies and courts for resolution. The numbers reported vary widely, depending on the definition of sexual harassment used (or not used) and the type of respondents surveyed, but they may shed some light on the historical level of harassment activity.

The Amount of Sexual Harassment Experienced

Respected estimates of the percentages of workers who have experienced sexual harassment have been made:

- A 1981 Merit System Protection Board study found that 42 percent of female government workers and 15 percent of male government respondees claimed to have experienced sexual harassment. In 1988, a questionnaire designed to update that study was sent to approximately 13,000 federal government employees considered to be a representative sample of the workplace population. Over 8,500 employees responded, with 42 percent of female respondees and 14 percent of male respondees reporting some form of unwelcome sexual occurrence between 1985 and 1987.[1]

- A 1988 survey of Fortune 500 companies sponsored by *Working Woman* magazine quantified activity from the corporate point of view. The 160 human resources executives who represented some 3.3 million employees indicated that almost all responding employers had received at least one sexual harassment complaint in the twelve-month period before the survey. Some 64 percent believed that the sexual harassment allegations they received were usually completely valid. Interestingly, more than 33 percent of responders reported that their corporations were sued for sexual harassment that year, with almost 25 percent characterizing their litigation activity as "repeated."[2]

- Sexual harassment claims brought to the Equal Employment Opportunity Commission numbered 4,400 in 1986 and jumped to 5,600 in 1990.[3] Informally, the commission reports a 25 percent increase for 1991 over 1990's sexual harassment caseload.

- An American Bar Association Foundation study of employment discrimination cases during the past twenty years found an almost 2,200 percent increase in employment discrimination cases in the federal courts, an increase ten times greater than all other civil litigation combined.[4] This is consistent with a five-year study of 2,000 employment-discrimination claims closed by the Ohio State Civil Rights Commission. In that study, 86 percent of the claims were filed under federal law and 14 percent under state statutes.[5]

- That same Ohio State Civil Rights Commission study found that charges of sexual harassment were present in about 5 percent of the 2,000 claims studied, but represented 25 percent of the 378 claims made for sex discrimination filed by both men (10%) and women (90%).[6]

- Of 155 women polled in the late 1970s by Working Women United Institute, 70 percent reported at least one incident of sexual harassment.[7]

Less formal surveys also give a clear sense of heightened awareness of sexual harassment as an issue:

- A January 1976 *Redbook* magazine questionnaire received more than 9,000 responses from women readers, with more than 92 percent characterizing sexual harassment as a problem for them, 50 percent as a serious problem. Nine of ten women reported experiencing one or more forms of unwelcome sexual attention on the job, with 75 percent calling their experience "embarrassing," "demeaning," or "intimidating."[8]

- In response to a question in the year-end 1989 issue of *People* magazine asking whether they have ever been sexually harassed at work, 25 percent of women readers and 10 percent of men readers told the magazine that they had.[9]

- A November 1991 survey by the American Management Association of its member companies found that 52 percent reported one or more allegations of sexual harassment within the last five years. In nearly 60 percent of the cases, some disciplinary action against the offender was taken. In 14 percent of those situations, that discipline took the form of termination. Interestingly, only half of the situations came to the attention of company management through formal channels; observation, informal reports, and anonymous notifications accounted for the rest.[10]

Complainant Characteristics

A small number of studies[11] has tried to profile the typical sexual harassment complainant as follows:

- *By age.* Most complainants are between 25 and 35 years of age; very few are over 45.
- *By marital status.* Almost half of complainants were single; less than a third were married. When widowed, divorced, or separated women were added to the single ranks, more than two-thirds of complainants were legally unattached.
- *By education.* Over 40 percent of complainants were high

school graduates; slightly over 50 percent had some college experience (13 percent) or had graduated from college (38 percent). Complainants with less than a high school or more than a college education both were minor contributors to the profile.

- *By occupation*. Unskilled workers and those in secretarial or clerical jobs accounted for 51 percent of complainants. Professionals such as doctors and lawyers accounted for only 3 percent. Being in a job traditionally performed by just one sex also seems to make alleged experiences more likely.

The Harassing Behavior

A strong consensus on the types of behavior considered by respondents to be sexual harassment emerges from the studies:

- The *Working Woman* survey found that 42 percent of complaints included teasing, jokes, or other remarks; 26 percent included touching, leaning over, or cornering; 17 percent included pressures for sexual favors; 12 percent included pressure for dates, and only one percent included actual or attempted serious physical contact.[12]
- In an examination of the sexual harassment charges filed with the Illinois State Equal Employment Opportunity Commission agency over a two-year period, most charges concerned minor "unwanted physical contact, offensive language, sexual propositions unlinked to threats or promises, and socialization or date requests."[13] Looking further to understand how these behaviors, considered less serious than others by the surveyers, resulted in high instances of litigation, researchers came upon an interesting corollary: Over 65 percent of charging parties alleging sexual harassment at work had been discharged and so were highly motivated to pursue their claims.[14] This finding was echoed by the more general results of the American Bar Association Foundation survey: Allegations of discrimination in firing now account for three out of

every four cases. Twenty years before, complaints arising from hiring decisions would have been in the clear majority.[15]

- In a study of sexual harassment cases after 1986, one researcher found that of sixty-five federal court cases on sexual harassment, only 4 percent based a claim entirely on supervisory threats or promises. In 75 percent of the cases reviewed, the sexual harassment claims concerned the nature of the working environment, with another 19 percent of the cases combining both types of allegations. Yet in 79 percent of the cases, the supervisor was the alleged harasser.[16]

- The *Working Woman* survey notes that 36 percent of complaints were made about immediate supervisors, another 26 percent about other people in power in the workplace, and 32 percent about coworker behavior.[17]

The Costs of Sexual Harassment

Some of the costs of sexual harassment are obvious and direct: costs of attorneys, awarded damages, or settlement costs. Others are less clear-cut, but may be even more significant when the effects of sexual harassment on the workplace are fully considered.

The Legal Expenses

Since sexual harassment claims are a form of sex discrimination prohibited by Title VII of the Civil Rights Act of 1964,[18] remedies under that legislation are restricted to such items as reinstatement or front pay, up to two years of back pay, attorney fees, and the possibility of injunctive relief. No jury trial and compensatory or punitive damages are available under Title VII.

However, more financial relief may be available under state statutes and certainly will be available to plaintiffs who augment their Title VII or state-law claims of sexual harassment with a wide variety of possible torts, or civil wrongs, to construct lawsuits with potentially formidable damages. These "tack-on" torts may include assault and battery, intentional or emotional infliction of mental distress, invasion of privacy, false imprisonment, negligent hiring, and quite frequently, defamation or damage to one's reputation or good name.

These torts can be particularly expensive for two reasons. First, an entire string of them can be added to the basic sexual harassment claim, limited only by the imagination of the plaintiff's attorney. Second, since all of these torts are forms of common-law negligence revamped in an employment setting, each of them carries the potential for a jury trial and for the assessment of punitive damages. Punitive damages are, like jury decisions, unpredictable and financially unplanned. How much money a given jury decides is enough to act as a deterrant to others is an unknown and, like most unknowns, is particularly uncomfortable for corporate senior managers to contemplate. Punitive damages are almost entirely up to the discretion of the given jury and jury decisions are not easily overturned, even if an employer considers the result to be outrageous.

Under the Civil Rights Act of 1991, sexual harassment claims will permit both compensatory and punitive damages, at least up to a set amount. Such liberalization in available money damages is expected to help fuel a further increase in these claims. Under the legislation, compensatory damages to make the claimant whole, such as expenses paid for medical treatment or for pain and suffering, will be available to victims of sexual harassment for the first time under federal law.

Punitive damages, however, will be available in sexual harrassment situations only for instances of *intentional* discrimination, not in cases of *disparate* (or adverse) *impact*. Disparate impact occurs when a policy or practice that is completely neutral on its face nevertheless results in adversely affecting a protected class. The classic example of disparate impact is in the administration of preemployment paper-and-pencil tests in which women and/or minority scores are consistently lower than those of white males using the same, neutral test instrument.

The amount of punitive damages will depend, not on the seriousness of the harassing activity itself, but on the number of employees in the workplace where the harassment took place. For companies with 15 to 100 employees, punitive damages can be a maximum of $50,000; employers of 101 to 200 employees will pay up to $100,000; employers of 201 to 500 employees will have their punitive damages exposure limited to $200,000, while employers of more than 500 employees will pay up to the punitive damages cap of $300,000.[19]

While many sexual harassment cases are settled out of court and many more are sealed against subsequent perusal, these sample damage awards give an indication of just how expensive a matter of sexual harassment may be:

- Five North Carolina women harassed by the same supervisor received $3.85 million in damages in 1988.[20]
- Also in 1988, K-Mart settled a sexual harassment claim for $3.2 million.[21]
- In 1987, a district court in Idaho granted $1.4 million to a former human resources manager who was fired for vigorously pursuing a sexual harassment investigation.[22]
- In 1990, a Ninth Circuit Court awarded $125,000 in compensatory and $500,000 in punitive damages to a woman alleging wrongful discharge owing to sexual harassment, along with intentional infliction of mental distress.[23]
- Also in 1990, a New York State court awarded $4 million in punitive damages to a former *Penthouse* pet who engaged in sexual affairs to benefit the magazine owner's business interests.[24]

Aside from amounts awarded to successful charging parties, an employer must also bear the cost of mounting a legal defense, whether a case goes to trial or settles out of court, and whether the case is of great or little merit. Legal expenses can range from a few thousand dollars to in excess of $200,000, depending on the situation and the firm selected to handle the legal aspects of the case. Internal expenses generated by the need to interview witnesses; gather and reproduce documents, files, production or operating records, and policy statements; and any and all other relevant materials may also prove to be unexpectedly costly. Clearly, a small fraction of those costs channeled into training and other preventive measures is money well spent.

Other Employer Costs

The nonlegal expenses caused by lower productivity, higher turnover, and poor morale can be even more considerable. The *Working Woman* survey estimated sexual harassment costs at $6,719,593 per company per year. That figure included such expenses as turnover costs, falloffs in production, and leaves of absence. It did not include the costs of litigation.[25] Even more striking is the estimate, considered as conservative, of the U.S. Merit Protection Board, of the costs of sexual harassment to the federal government from May 1985 to May 1987: $267 million. Government estimates include the cost of replacing employees who leave because of sexual harassment, sick-leave payments to employees who are absent from work because of sexual harassment concerns, as well as the cost of reduced productivity, both individually and in groups.[26] In one nationwide survey of women who reported experiencing sexual harassment at work, 42 percent felt compelled by continued harassment or postcomplaint retaliation to quit their jobs.[27]

To many commentators, the hidden expenses of turnover, sick leave and absenteeism, and decreased effectiveness are the real corporate issues; indeed, they may directly affect not only how corporations respond to women bringing sexual harassment allegations to their attention, but may be significant factors in shaping their views of women in the workplace. For example:

> Stereotypical perceptions are that women are less suited than men to many jobs; women do not stay with their jobs; women lack education and experience; women are absent from work more often than men; women are unable to travel; women would not be accepted in positions of authority, and women are incapable of making decisions based on fact and logic. The factual basis of some of these stereotypes

are (*sic*) often the very result of sexual harassment. For example, sexually harassed women more often than not leave their jobs, thereby "not staying with their jobs." If they stay and try to cope with the sexual harassment, they will probably be absent more often and their productivity may understandably decrease.[28]

While not easily quantified, these costs are just as real—and just as debilitating to the organization and to society as a whole.

The Changing Look of the Workplace

Historically, the typical American worker was male and Caucasian, and he worked his entire adult life for perhaps only one or two organizations until retirement. The last twenty-five years have radically changed that picture. Confronted with the need to meet increasing expenses and concerned about meeting self-actualization ideals, American women have rushed to enter the work force, drastically altering both work and family patterns. By 1988, 52 percent of all American women worked outside of the home, with 75 percent of them in their childbearing years. The fastest-growing segment of the work force now consisted of women with children under six years of age. About 60 percent of school-age children had working mothers.[29]

Projections on the composition of the work force of the future, or the work force in the year 2000, only increase the percentage of women (and more minorities, as well) in the job market, made capable by higher education and greater work experience of performing a wide variety of functions at all levels in a typical organization. Between 1985 and the year 2000, women are expected to represent 42 percent of new entrants into the labor market, while white males will contribute only 15 percent of new work force members.[30]

Women no longer are always secretaries or clerical support personnel, but are colleagues and coworkers with whom meaningful professional relationships must be built and nurtured. Men have had a lot of adjusting to do in the workplace as well as at home, as women have invented new roles to meet new needs. Men and women have learned to meet together, to plan together, to lunch together, to work on assignments together, to work out at the gym together, to travel together.

Joining this demographic revolution are some changes in the way work, socialization, and the interaction of sexes are now viewed. In their efforts to exceed past income levels and rise within the organization, both men and women have increased the amount of time and attention that work receives in their lives. Instead of working a forty-hour week, workers try to become more upwardly mobile by consistently working seventy, eighty, or even more hours per week.

Investing that amount of time and physical and mental energy in their working lives leaves very little for the social aspects of living. Given the nature of these trends and the changing demographics of the workplace, it is not surprising that work is the primary daily social experience for a large number of men and women. Under these conditions, the workplace also becomes the primary area for meeting new people of the opposite sex, and for exploring these new relationships in social or quasi-social settings frequently related to work. It is not surprising that sexual liaisons develop, and that men and women have difficulty keeping their working and nonworking lives separate. Miscommunications, misunderstandings, and just plain confusion sometimes result, as they do in any social relationship. The major difference is that, at work, the vagaries of a relationship may well have an impact on the workplace, as couples struggle to find the line between permissible interaction and acts of sexual harassment.

NOTES

1. U.S. Merit Systems Protection Board, "Sexual Harassment in the Federal Government: An Update" (June, 1988), pp. 1–2.

2. Diane Feldman, "Harassment Touches All in Workplace," *Management Review* (April 1989), pp. 8–9.
3. "Ending Sexual Harassment: Business is Getting the Message," *Business Week* (March 18, 1991), pp. 98–100.
4. Mark Hansen, "Study Shows Job Bias Changing," *American Bar Association Journal* (May 1991), p. 34.
5. William M. Slonaker and Ann C. Wendt, "No Job Is Safe From Discrimination," *HR Magazine* (October 1991), pp. 69–70.
6. Ibid.
7. Alice Montgomery, "Sexual Harassment in the Workplace: A Practitioner's Guide to Tort Actions," 10 GARDEN STATE U. L. REV. 879 n.2 (1980).
8. As reported in Claudia Laks Cerutti, "Differing Standards of Employer Liability for Sexual Harassment of Working Women," 27 ARIZONA L. REV., 158 n.20 (1985).
9. *People*, December 25, 1989.
10. American Management Association press release, November 21, 1991.
11. David E. Terpstra, "Who Gets Sexually Harassed?" *Personnel Administrator* (March 1989), pp. 84–88, 111. Also see U.S. Merit Protection Board study, *supra* note 1.
12. Norma R. Fritz, "Sexual Harassment and the Working Woman," *Personnel* (February 1989), pp. 4–8.
13. Terpstra, "Who Gets Harrassed?", p. 85.
14. Ibid.
15. Hansen, "Study Shows Job Bias."
16. Clifford M. Koen, Jr., "Sexual Harassment Claims Stem From a Hostile Work Environment," *Personnel* (August 1990), pp. 91–92.
17. Fritz, "Sexual Harassment."
18. Civil Rights Act of 1964, Pub. L. No. 88-352 §703, 38 Stat. 241, 255 (1964), 42 U.S.C. §20003-2(a) (1982).
19. Timothy Noah and Albert R. Karr, "What New Civil Rights Law Will Mean," *Wall Street Journal*, November 4, 1991, pp. B1, B10.
20. "Harassment Case Yields $3.85 Million," *Charlotte Observer*, October 12, 1988.

21. "Sexual Harassment Plagues Companies," Johnson City Press (AP Wire), November 24, 1988, p. 24.
22. *O'Dell v. Basabe,* Idaho 4th District Court, No. 88574, June 3, 1987.
23. *Dias v. Sky Chefs, Inc.,* No. 89–35,778 (9th Cir. 1990), FEP Cases 852.
24. *Thoreson v. Penthouse International, Ltd. and Robert Guccione,* 149 Misc. 2d 150, 563 N.Y.S.2d 968.
25. Fritz, "Sexual Harassment."
26. U.S. Merit Protection Board, "Sexual Harassment."
27. "Unemployment Compensation Benefits for the Victim of Work-Related Sexual Harassment," 3 HARV. WOMEN'S L. J. 179, n.37 (Spring 1980).
28. Cerutti, "Differing Standards."
29. Elizabeth Erlich and Susan B. Garland, "For American Business, A New World of Workers," *Business Week* (September 19, 1988), pp. 112–13.
30. Bruce Nussbaum, "Needed: Human Capital," *Business Week* (September 19, 1988), pp. 102–103.

3

What Sexual Harassment Is, and What It Is Not

In 1964, Congress passed what can arguably be described as the single most important piece of employment legislation ever adopted. Based on the notion that employees should not be adversely affected by personal characteristics that have nothing to do with skills, abilities, or job performance, Title VII of the Civil Rights Act of 1964 prohibits all forms of discrimination on the basis of race, color, religion, national origin, and sex, in all aspects of employment:

> It shall be an unlawful employment practice for an employer: (1) to fail or refuse to hire or to discharge any individual, or otherwise to discriminate against any individual with respect to his compensation, terms, conditions or privileges of employment because of such individual's race, color, religion, sex, or national origin or (2) to limit, segregate, or classify his employees or applicants for employment in any way which would deprive or tend to deprive any individual of employment opportunities or otherwise adversely affect his status as an employee, because of such individual's race, color, religion, sex, or national origin.[1]

Harassment on the basis of sex is a violation of Title VII, but it took several years for a judicial consensus to develop regarding its parameters.

Initial court reaction to claims of sexual harassment was not entirely favorable. Early cases characterized supervisory sexual advances as simply "satisfying a personal urge."[2] Judges worried about upsetting what they considered to be the natural order of the workplace, noting that if sexual harassment allegations were recognized, "flirtations of the smallest order would give rise to liability. . . . The attraction of males to females and females to males is a natural sex phenomenon and it is probable that this attraction plays at least a subtle part in most personnel decisions."[3]

The tide began to turn with the 1976 case of *Williams v. Saxbe.*[4] Williams, a Justice Department employee, claimed her supervisor terminated her employment after she had refused to accede to repeated requests for sexual favors.

In 1980, the Equal Employment Opportunity Commission issued its guidelines on sexual harassment and its now famous definition delineating the two types of illegal conduct:

> Unwelcome sexual advances, requests for sexual favors, and other verbal or physical conduct of a sexual nature constitute sexual harassment when (1) submission to such conduct is made either explicitly or implicitly a term or condition of an individual's employment, (2) submission to or rejection of such conduct by an individual is used as the basis for employment decisions affecting such individual, or (3) such conduct has the purpose or effect of unreasonably interfering with an individual's work performance or creating an intimidating, hostile, or offensive work environment.[5]

Once quid pro quo sexual harassment was firmly established in case law, courts began to grapple with the more subtle issues of hostile-environment sexual harassment. Relying on a 1971 racial harassment case, *Rogers v. EEOC,*[6] for precedent, courts began to recognize workplace-atmosphere issues as separate claims, regardless of whether the harasser was a supervisor. In 1981, in *Bundy v. Jackson,*[7] for example, when the plaintiff's supervisor repeatedly invited her to spend afternoons with him in his apartment and another supervisor invited her to a motel room and on a Bahamas trip, she complained to higher management. The senior manager dismissed her complaint, saying "any man in his right mind would want to rape you" and went on to proposition the plaintiff himself.

It was not until 1986 that the Supreme Court ruled on its one and only sexual harassment case: *Meritor Savings Bank v. Vinson.*[8] Hired by the bank as a teller-trainee, Mechelle Vinson advanced on the basis of her abilities to the position of assistant branch manager before her ultimate termination for excessive use of sick leave. About a year later, Vinson sued the bank and Sidney Taylor, her supervisor, alleging hostile-environment sexual harassment. Vinson claimed that during her four years at the bank, she had sex with Taylor some forty or fifty times. He also followed her into the ladies room, fondled her in front of coworkers, and raped her several times. While the bank had an antidiscrimination policy and a stated complaint procedure, Vinson did not use the internal process, claiming that she feared reprisals. In their defense, Taylor and the bank alleged that the ongoing relationship was entirely voluntary and that no liability should attach, since there was no notice to the employer. Despite the length of the relationship and the lack of notice, the Supreme Court recognized Vinson's hostile-environment claim in a landmark decision having far-reaching implications for employers.

The Two Basic Requirements
for Sexual Harassment

The Equal Employment Opportunity Commission definition sets two general criteria for sexual harassment: that the conduct in question, whether physical or verbal, is both unwelcome and of a sexual nature.

The Concept of Unwelcome Conduct

Whether or not conduct is unwelcome is a critical concept. Conduct is not welcome when it is unsolicited, when the victim has done nothing to incite it, and when the victim views that conduct as undesirable or offensive. Simply because a woman acquiesces to sexual demands—or participates in a sexual relationship, even for an extended period of time—conclusions cannot be automatically drawn about whether or not she welcomed that conduct. The Supreme Court in *Vinson* drew a clear distinction between conduct that was voluntary and conduct that was welcome. Mechelle Vinson voluntarily (no one put a gun to her head) participated in a sexual relationship with her supervisor for several years, involving forty or fifty acts of sexual intercourse, and yet was able to successfully state that the conduct was unwelcome (undesirable or offensive) to her, that she acquiesced only out of fear of losing her job and fear of retaliatory action should she refuse to comply with Taylor's sexual demands.

Whether or not conduct is welcome can be judged by what women do and say, what reactions they have to sexual conduct, and what kinds of interactions they have with the particular individual they claim has harassed them. Questions about unwelcome behavior are, like all sexual harassment issues, fact based and confined to the relationship at issue; unwelcomeness is not a general concept. For example, in *Sardigal v. St. Louis National Stockyards Co.*,[9] the plaintiff's assertion that her alleged harasser's conduct was unwelcome was held not credible when she visited him in the hospital and at his brother's home, and allowed him into her home alone at night after the alleged harassment occurred. Similarly, in *Gan v. Kepro Circuit Systems*,[10] the plaintiff's use of vulgar language; her initiation of conversations on sexual subjects with coworkers, including inquiries to males about their marital and extramarital sex lives; and her willingness to discuss her own sexual experiences led the court to reject her claim of hostile-environment harassment. Indeed, the court found any sexual advances made to be "prompted by her own sexual aggressiveness and her own sexually explicit conversations."[11]

A close inquiry into the specific levels of interpersonal contact between the parties, and the timing of those interactions, is necessary to establish whether behavior is welcome or not. The Supreme Court recognized this issue in its *Meritor* decision when it permitted the introduction of evidence on Vinson's dress, language, and behavior in the workplace to bolster defense contentions that the behavior at issue was both voluntary and welcome.

A central inquiry of any investigation must, then, be whether the alleged harassing activity was unwelcome rather than involuntary, and how the parties should have known that.

Welcomeness is frequently an issue when women have participated in a certain level of joking, teasing, or verbal repartee but feel uncomfortable or offended when the level of such sexually oriented discussion escalates. It is also a key factor in situations involving the end of consensual sexual relationships. In both of these common circumstances, it is even more important to provide notice to others that behavior that may once have been fine is now unwelcome and offensive. Otherwise, coworkers and former lovers may be entitled to rely on past behavior to assume conduct is still as welcome as it ever was.

The Sexual Nature of Conduct

The requirement that sexually harassing conduct, whether physical or verbal, be of a sexual nature is typically fulfilled by such frequently cited behaviors as propositions, comments on the sexual areas of a woman's body, dirty jokes, pictures of nude or sexually suggestive individuals, and sexually oriented cartoons. However, the requirement that conduct be of a sexual nature can also be fulfilled through nonsexual verbal and physical behavior caused by the gender of the individual being harassed. In other words, "but for" the sex of the individual, the harassing behavior would not have occurred.

A good example of such behavior is *Hall v. Gus Construction Co.*[12] Here, the three female plaintiffs were subjected to conduct designed to make their work lives difficult and to let them know that women were not welcome on the job site. That behavior included urinating in the gas tank of the plaintiff's car, locking the door of the restroom at the job site and refusing to stop on the road so the plaintiff could go to the bathroom, letting a dangerous condition persist in the plaintiff's truck until a male employee used it, and so on. These acts were not sexually oriented in the same way that sexual comments and nude displays are, yet they are sexual in nature because they are based on the gender of the victim.

The commission's definition goes on to describe the two types of conduct considered to be sexual harassment: quid pro quo and hostile environment. Employers need to familiarize themselves with the characteristics of both types of sexual harassment—their similarities, their differences, and their implications for employer liability.

A Closer Look at Quid Pro Quo

Quid pro quo ("this for that") sexual harassment involves the exchange of a job benefit for express or implied sexual favors: "If you want that raise, that promotion . . . if you want to keep your job, you'll have to sleep with me." Typical quid pro quo situations are suggestions of unnecessary after-hours work or out-of-town travel, statements like "It would really help your career to work more closely with me," or "If you want that assignment, you're going to have to be nice to me."

Characteristics of Quid Pro Quo

▪ To be in a position to make these kinds of job-related threats or promises, the harasser needs to be in a position of authority over the harassed employee. In this form of sexual harassment, the accused is always the immediate supervisor or someone else who has the actual or apparent authority to affect terms and conditions of employment.

▪ The charging party must be able to show money damages to successfully claim quid pro quo harassment. Since the terms and conditions of employment are always directly involved, money damages are usually easy to demonstrate. Damages can include monies associated with lost promotion opportunities, missed raises, or in the event of actual or constructive discharge, the full value of wages and benefits lost less an amount the charging party might reasonably have earned had she pursued another job opportunity.

▪ Unlike hostile-environment harassment, one incident can be enough in quid pro quo situations.

Implications for Employer Liability

Historically, the Equal Employment Opportunity Commission has taken the position that quid pro quo sexual harassment always results in strict liability to the employer, regardless of whether the employer knew the harassment was occurring and despite the existence of prohibitive policy statements, a proper complaint procedure, extensive management training, or a general atmosphere of disapproval. The theory creating this automatic liability is known as *respondeat superior*, meaning that the master is responsible for the acts of his servant and the principal for the acts of his agent. Since supervisory personnel have the power to hire, fire, reward, and punish, their sexual advances to their employees are fundamental abuses of the power conferred on them by the corporation. Rather than sex, quid pro quo harassment is really about the power of bosses (mostly male) over subordinates (mostly female) and the abuse of that power.

Agreeing with the commission, every appeals court that has ruled on the issue has automatically held employers liable for the sexual harassment of their supervisors when that behavior resulted in a tangible loss for the employee.

Thus, the message to employers is clear: Select and train your managers well, because their actions will be considered to be your own; do everything in your power to make the organization's prohibition of sexual harassment clear, widely communicated, and fully enforced.

Supervisors and managers must come to understand that serious disciplinary sanctions will be leveled if they abuse their authority over their employees. The additional specter of financial hardship, through personal liability or the award of punitive damages (generally not covered by corporate or individual insurance policies) as well as the possibility of criminal sanctions should circumstances warrant, is a serious behaviorial check, but only if it is fully and regularly communicated.

A Closer Look at Hostile-Environment Harassment

The situations generally involved in hostile-environment claims are less clear-cut. Here, typical situations are lewd jokes or comments, displays of explicit or sexually suggestive material, or repeated requests for a sexual or dating relationship.

Characteristics of Hostile-Environment Harassment

▪ Harassers may be anyone in the workplace: supervisors, coworkers, customers, suppliers, or visitors. The employer is responsible for what happens on company premises or at off-premises, work-related functions such as dinners, parties, or business trips.

▪ Unlike quid pro quo harassment, one isolated incident is rarely enough. Hostile-environment harassment requires that the offensive conduct be continuous, frequent, repetitive, and part of an overall pattern, rather than one event or even several isolated incidents separated by some length of time.

▪ Money damages do not need to be demonstrated and, in fact, may not exist. For this reason, supervisors who have made no direct link to the terms and conditions of the victim's job, who have not attempted to make the employee's behavior something to be exchanged for a concrete job benefit, or her refusal of something to be changed for a concrete job benefit, may be charged under a theory of hostile-environment harassment.

▪ The conduct must rise to such a level that the charging party's job peformance is interfered with or her working atmosphere is rendered abusive. Title VII is not designed to eliminate all expression of human sexuality in the workplace; it prohibits only conduct that is unwelcome and that affects a woman in her role as a worker. To determine whether or not these conditions have been met, the Equal Employment Opportunity Commission recommends consideration of these factors:

> (1) the extent to which the conduct affected the employee's terms and conditions of employment; (2) whether the conduct was repeated or isolated; (3) whether the conduct was intended or perceived seriously or in jest; and (4), the degree to which the conduct is contrary to community standards.[13]

These factors emphasize the importance of the unique facts and circumstances involved in every situation, including such intangibles as generally held attitudes and perceptions about sex at work that might vary substantially from New York City to Small Town, U.S.A., to the norms and mores common to the industry involved. A hello kiss on the cheek may be an entirely usual and expected form of greeting between strangers in the entertainment world, and entirely inappropriate between coworkers on Wall Street.

The commission also looks at who the alleged harasser is (the supervisor or a nonsupervisory employee) and whether the victim was singled out or the alleged conduct was also directed at others.[14]

- To successfully bring a claim for hostile-environment sexual harassment after *Meritor*, a claimant must show not only that she herself was affected and offended by the sexual conduct but that an objective third party—a reasonable person—would also have been offended. Before the 1986 Supreme Court decision, companies had to deal with a notion of sexual harassment that was pretty much "in the eye of the beholder," even when the plaintiffs' super-sensitivities were offended by conduct regarded as trivial by coworkers. In *Meritor*, the Supreme Court created a much more objective standard: In that jurisdiction, would a reasonable person have found the conduct offensive as well? Equal Employment Opportunity Commission guidelines also urge investigators to view situations as would a reasonable person in the same circumstances, taking the perspective of the victim into account. The commission's standard, therefore, tends to be somewhat higher than the simple, reasonable person's view.

In 1991, a number of courts (Michigan, Florida, and California) have replaced their reasonable *person* standard with a reasonable *woman* standard.[15] This latest trend reflects judicial recognition of the fact that men and women tend to view sexual matters in very different ways and that what may be trivial to a reasonable male may be quite serious to a reasonable female. According to the Ninth Circuit Court, the reasonable-person standard tends to be male-biased and to ignore the experiences of women in a systematic way: "Men tend to view some forms of sexual harassment as harmless social interactions to which only over-sensitive women would object . . . the characteristically male view depicts sexual harassment as comparatively harmless amusement."[16]

In making its determination, the Florida court relied on expert testimony about the differences in perspectives of the two sexes. The research cited found that almost two-thirds of males expected to be flattered by a sexual approach in the workplace, while only 15 percent expected to be insulted. For female workers, the proportions were reversed.[17]

Under this new standard of reasonableness, much less in the way of offensive behavior may be needed for a finding of hostile-environment sexual harassment if a reasonable person of the same sex as the complainant considers the conduct sufficient to alter a condition of employment or create an abusive environment.

Implications for Employer Liability

Employer liability in hostile-environment situations is a good deal less clear-cut than when harassment is of the quid pro quo variety. Liability depends on a close analysis of the individual facts of each particular situation, as well as these general principles:

- Whether or not the employer had notice of the harassment. Without notice, liability will likely not attach. Notice may be actual (an employee's complaint, a copy of a filed Equal

Employment Opportunity Commission charge, an informal chat with an eyewitness) or constructive (the employer is not actually told, but the circumstances are such that the employer should have known of the harassment). Constructive notice might be conspicuous displays of raucous pictures or clippings from sexual magazines, well-known levels of sexual jokes and teasing in a certain department, gossip or rumor about the repetitive attempts of a particular supervisor to date his subordinates—in short, anything that is there to see or there to hear, and therefore should have been noticed by the employer.

- What the employer does about the sexual harassing activity once it comes to the company's attention. If the employer investigated and resolved the situation appropriately within a reasonable period of time, liability may be considerably lessened, and in some circumstances, it may be eliminated altogether.

- Whether or not the employer has developed and communicated a strong policy prohibiting sexual harassment and has provided an effective procedure for bringing harassment concerns to the company's attention. While a policy and procedures statement will not insulate an employer from potential liability, it does help establish good faith and raise questions about employee claims not brought for internal resolution.

- The identity of the harasser. If the alleged harasser is not a supervisory employee, the Equal Employment Opportunity Commission and the courts are in agreement that liability attaches only if an employer who had actual or constructive knowledge fails to respond with prompt and effective action to address the harassment situation.

In the latter case, however, if the harasser is also the employee's supervisor, liability is affected by the jurisdiction involved. Since the Supreme Court's consideration of the issue of employer liability in a hostile-environment case in *Meritor* did not result in the kind of "bright line" pronouncement that many commentators and lower court judges were hoping to hear, the various courts have therefore interpreted the *Meritor* decision in varying ways. Instead of applying strict liability, or using the master-servant theory, the Court looked to the general principles of agency law to determine whether the employer was liable for the acts of his agent.[18]

Under common-law agency principles, an employer's liability for its agents' acts is restricted to conduct that falls within the scope of the agents' employment. While there will no doubt be many attempts to argue that harassment is never within the supervisor's scope of employment, and therefore the supervisor is never acting for his employer when he engages in this kind of activity, it is the employer's grant of actual or apparent authority to affect an employee's terms and conditions of employment that allows the behavior to occur. Given the historic strict-liability standard for supervisory behavior and the tendency of the commission and the courts to hold supervisors to a higher level of behavior, it is likely that the supervisor's actions will be imputed to the employer and liability will result under theories of agency just as surely as under respondeat superior.

In the wake of *Meritor,* the various circuit courts have not adopted a single standard for employer liability when the alleged harasser in a hostile-environment case is the supervisor. In the Sixth, Seventh, and Tenth Circuits, for example, the pros and cons of the agency theory of liability form the center of the court's inquiry.[19] The Tenth and Eleventh Circuits tend to hold supervisors to a higher standard because they are supervisors.[20] The First and Fourth Circuits focus on the issue of notice and subsequent employer action in determining liability.[21]

The Equal Employment Opportunity Commission, revising its prior strict liability stand for supervisory behavior regardless of the context, has issued guidelines that seem to blend these two theories. For the commission, employers are liable when they have invested the harassing supervisor with actual or apparent authority and they knew or should have known the harassment occurred.[22]

Clearly, the facts and the issues of notice and authority are key elements in determining liability, and they should be the central focus of any investigation of hostile-environment claims. Employers should be aware that liability for supervisory actions under these circumstances is still evolving, and therefore they should pay attention to all of the elements agencies and courts have found to be important.

Careful drafting and communication of a policy against sexual harassment that provides an effective and credible internal complaint-resolution process is a key preventive measure that may also significantly reduce the employer's overall liability. The Equal Employment Opportunity Commission takes the position that employees may reasonably believe that sexual harassment is condoned in a workplace that has no such policy statement and effective complaint procedure. At the same time, investigators have focused on why internal systems were bypassed by employees claiming to have been sexually harassed, as a measure of the employees' credibility.[23] This is clearly an area in which employers want to do everything possible to encourage notice, so that liability can be cut off, or at least minimized, through prompt action.

Same-Sex Harassment

Sexual harassment can also occur between members of the same sex, since the harassment occurs because of the sex of the victim regardless of the victim's sexual preference. For example, in *Wright v. Methodist Youth Services, Inc.*,[24] a male employee's discharge after rejection of his male supervisor's sexual advances is recognizable under Title VII. A female employee's demotion for refusal of her female supervisor's sexual advances also established a Title VII claim.[25]

Although Title VII does not prohibit discrimination on the basis of sexual preference (many state and local statutes do, however), it does prohibit sexual harassment as a form of sex discrimination between employees of the same sex just as it does when both sexes are involved. Employers need to be aware of the possibility of same-sex harassment activity from supervisors and coworkers, regardless of whether the preference is shared by the harassee. The same standards of liability and the same theoretical analysis apply.

Using Workers Compensation to Limit Liability

Workers compensation statutes usually provide an exclusive remedy for employees who are injured on the job. The exclusivity, precluding common law or any other claims, affects only the corporate liability of employers, not the personal liability of individual supervisors or coworkers. It also holds only as long as the employer does not direct or instigate the injurious conduct. In some jurisdictions, such as Florida, Illinois, Maine, Wisconsin, and New York,[26] corporate employers have successfully asserted this exclusivity provision as an affirmative defense, effectively using the state statutes on job-related injuries to cut off the bulk of potential liability.

Some jurisdictions, however, have considered and rejected this argument, including New Jersey, Montana, California, New York (which seems to go both ways on this issue), Colorado, and Virginia, which passed a statute removing the exclusivity provision for sexual assault injuries.[27] Since these issues are frequently in flux, it may be worthwhile to discuss individual situations with legal counsel as well as with insurers.

What Sexual Harassment Is

To summarize, for conduct to be sexual harassment it must be unwelcome and affect the terms and conditions of employment. As a practical matter, that conduct can include:

- Derogatory or vulgar comments about someone's gender, physical anatomy, or characteristics
- Sexually suggestive or vulgar language
- Threats of physical harm
- Sexually oriented or suggestive pictures, posters, magazines, or other materials
- Touching someone in a sexually suggestive way, or in a way calculated to invade her personal space
- Touching of another's breasts, genital areas, or derriere

And What It's Not

A number of misconceptions of sexual harassment have found their way into the popular press, on television and radio, and in newspapers and magazines. Men in particular have begun to voice fears that sexual-harassment concerns effectively prohibit any kind of social interaction between the sexes, even to the point of polite compliments on a woman's dress or asking what she did during the weekend. From both a legal and a practical perspective, these fears are unfounded, the product of misinformation or a lack of the kind of specific information found in this chapter.

Sexual harassment is not involved in normal, pleasant, friendly, or even mildly flirtatious interactions, as long as no reasonable person (woman) is offended. Common courtesy, common sense, and a habit of close observation of others' reactions to what is said and done go a long way in achieving a friendly work environment where both sexes can enjoy each other's company in an atmosphere free of sexual harassment.

NOTES

1. Civil Rights Act of 1964, Pub. L. No. 88–352 §703, 38 Stat. 241, 255 (1964), 42 U.S.C. §20003–2(a)(1982).
2. *Corne v. Bausch & Lomb, Inc.*, 390 F. Supp. 161 (D. Ariz. 1975).
3. *Miller v. Bank of America*, 418 F. Supp. 233 (N.D. Cal. 1976).
4. *Williams v. Saxbe*, 413 F. Supp. 654 (D.C. Cir. 1976).
5. 29 C.F.R. §1604.11(a).
6. 454 F. 2d 234 (5th Cir. 1971).
7. 641 F. 2d 934 (D.C. Cir. 1981).
8. 106 S. Ct. 2399 (1986).
9. 41 EPD §36, 613 (S.D. Ill. 1986).
10. 27 EPD §32, 279 (E.D. Mo. 1982).
11. Op. cit. at 23, 648.
12. 46 FEP Cases 573 (8th Cir. 1988).
13. 29 C.F.R. §1604.11 (1988).

14. Ibid.
15. *Radtke v. Everett,* Michigan Ct. of Appeals 121611, May 20, 1991; *Robinson v. Jacksonville Shipyards,* 86–927–CIV-J–12 (M.D. Fla. Jan. 18, 1991); *Ellison v. Brady,* 924 F. 2d 871 (9th Cir. 1991).
16. *Ellison v. Brady,* note 15.
17. *Robinson v. Jacksonville Shipyards,* note 15.
18. 106 S. Ct. 2399 (1986).
19. Eric J. Wallach and Jean Simonoff Marx, "Courts Draw the Liability Line on Work Place Sex Harassment," *National Law Journal* (February 13, 1989), pp. 21–22.
20. Ibid.
21. Ibid.
22. 29 C.F.R. §1604.11 (1988).
23. Ibid.
24. 511 F. Supp. 307, 309–10 (N.D. Ill. 1981).
25. 30 FEP 223, 223 (N.D. Ill. 1980).
26. *Studstill v. Borg-Warner Lerasing,* 806 F. 2d 1005, 1007 (11th Cir. 1986); *Bailey v. Unocal Corp.,* 700 F. Supp. 396 (N.D. Ill. 1988); *Knox v. Combines Insur. Co. of Amer.,* 542A.2d 363 (Me. 1988); *Zabkowicz v. West Bend Co.,* 789 F. 2d 544 (7th Cir. 1986); *Hart v. Sullivan,* 84 A.D. 2d 865, 445 N.Y.S. 2d 40 (3rd Dept. 1981), aff'd, 55 N.Y. 2d 1011, 449 N.Y.S. 2d 481 (1982).
27. *Cremen v. Harrah's Marina Hotel Casino,* 680 F. Supp. 150 (D.N.J. 1988); *Oedewaldt v. J. C. Penney Co.,* 687 F. Supp. 517, 519 (D. Mont. 1988), *Hart v. Nat'l Mortgage & Land Co.,* 189 Cal. App. 3d 1420, 1432, 235 Cal. Rptr, 68, 75 (4th Dist. 1987); *Thompson v. Maimonides Med. Ctr.,* 86 A. D. 2d 867, 447 N.Y.S. 2d 308 (2d Dept. 1982); *Spoon v. American Agri-culturalist, Inc.,* 120 A. D. 2d 857, 860, 502 N.Y.S. 2d 296, 299 (3d Dept. 1986); *Bennett v. Furr's Cafeterias, Inc.,* 549 F. Supp. 887, 890–91 (D. Colo. 1982); Va. Code Ann. §65.1–23.1 (1988).

4

Sexual Harassment—or Paramour Preference?

Sexual harassment allegations can frequently have an impact on more than just the two individuals most directly involved. Increasingly at issue are the rights of a variety of third parties. The Equal Employment Opportunity Commission's 1988 Guidelines on Discrimination Because of Sex opens the door to third-party claims caused by sexual favoritism:

> Where employment opportunities or benefits are granted because of an individual's submission to the employer's sexual advances or requests for sexual favor, the employer may be held liable for unlawful sex discrimination against other persons who were qualified for but were denied that employment opportunity or benefit.[1]

In the eyes of the commission and the courts, a certain amount of favoritism based on such things as sexual attraction or an ongoing personal relationship that includes sex or the expectation of sex, is only a natural fact of human life. Indeed, the courts have coined a novel label for the situation in which supervisors with job-related benefits to bestow bypass equally or better qualified staff members to confer the advantage on the object of their affections: *paramour preference*. But under some circumstances, the guidelines create a cause of action for third parties who were harmed because of such a liaison at work.

Since the guidelines were issued, employers have grappled with nebulous questions of sexual mores, privacy issues, and gradations of workplace behavior usually found only in "Dear Abby" columns. The courts were equally confused, rendering decisions on both sides of the issue and for various reasons. Because of these inconsistent decisions, and the good deal of confusion the topic has generated, in 1990 the Equal Employment Opportunity Commission issued a policy statement to clarify the employer's responsibilities and the rights of third-party claimants.

While this area of the law continues to evolve, in general these factors will be important ones in third-party claims and, therefore, are matters employers need to be aware of and prepared to act on.

The Nature of the Sexual Relationship

Many courts draw a distinction between consensual and non-consensual (that is, illegal situations involving acts of sexual harassment) arrangements. If a manager with a promotion opportunity available chooses to bestow that job benefit on a subordinate he is sexually involved with, one key issue is whether that involvement is mutually welcome.

If the relationship is one of harasser and harassed employee, then the other employees qualified for the promotion but bypassed in favor of the harassed employee may well have third-party claims of sexual harassment that, in fact, possibly blend allegations of both hostile environment and quid pro quo. The theory at work here is simple: Both men and women have been injured as a result of the discriminatory treatment of the coerced employee by being denied the opportunity of a job benefit on the basis of sex.

However, if the promoting manager and his favorite subordinate enjoy an ordinary, garden-variety affair with no unwelcome aspects to it, then many courts feel that it is only natural and eminently predictable that the manager will prefer his paramour to the other candidates. No claim will be possible because all of the individuals, whether women or men, are not disadvantaged because of their genders but because of the intimate relationship the manager enjoys with one favored person.

The Extent and Frequency of the Preference

For paramour preference to hold, the commission requires that it be limited to isolated instances that, while unfair, are not illegal. For instance, in *DeCintio v. Westchester County Medical Center*,[2] seven male respiratory therapists were passed over for promotion through imposition of a new job requirement that only the woman romantically involved with the hiring manager possessed. The district court for the Southern District of New York agreed that the new requirement was a subterfuge to allow for the hiring of the woman and, therefore, that the seven males were paid less for performing essentially equivalent work, a violation of both Title VII and the Equal Pay Act.

The Second Circuit reversed the decision, however, finding that the male therapists were bypassed not because they were male but because the administrator preferred his paramour. Had the group bypassed included a woman, she would have been bypassed for the same reason.

In this case, as in cases where preference is an isolated event, there is no nexus between the entirely consensual, mutually welcomed relationship and the giving or receiving of a tangible job benefit. Without that nexus, Title VII does not apply.

This same line of reasoning is found in a recent California Court of Appeals decision under California's Fair Employment and Housing Act, *Fisher v. San Pedro Peninsula Hospital*.[3] Fisher, an operating-room nurse, made several attempts to end the harassment of coworkers by a hospital physician. She was ostracized by her coworkers, began to suffer physical symptoms as a result of the doctor's conduct, and ultimately resigned, contending that her working conditions had been made intolerable. Because Fisher was not alleging harassing conduct aimed directly at her, but rather at her coworkers, the court believed that she "should be required to plead sufficient facts to establish a nexus between the alleged sexual harassment of others, her observation of that conduct and the work context in which it occurred." Fisher must show "that her working environment was permeated by sexual harassment."[4]

An Atmosphere of Harassment

If preferential allegations are coupled with a generally hostile environment, even the consensual nature of the paramour relationship may not be enough to prevent a successful third-party claim for sex discrimination based on the theory that sex had become a condition of employment. For example, in *Toscana v. Nimmo*,[5] the plaintiff was an assistant in medical administration and one of five applicants for an administrative position at a veterans' hospital. The individual given the preferential treatment was engaged in a consensual affair with her supervisor, but his behavior was generally abusive. A self-described womanizer, the supervisor regularly called female employees at home, touched them suggestively, and made sexual comments, a pattern of behavior that factored significantly in the court's decision in favor of the plaintiff.

How Widespread the Favoritism Is

If *DeCintio* is at one end of the spectrum, then *Broderick v. Ruder*[6] is at the other. An office of the Securities and Exchange Commission was a repository for a host of consensual relationships. The plaintiff, a staff attorney there, alleged that two of her superiors were involved in sexual relationships with two secretaries, and had rewarded them with promotions, cash, and other job benefits. There also was involvement between a third superior and another staff attorney, as well as isolated instances of harassment directed at the plaintiff. (For example, at an office party a drunken supervisor untied her top and kissed her.)

On these facts, the court had no difficulty in finding that a hostile environment had been created, regardless of the fact that all of the relationships the plaintiff had identified were entirely consensual. The issue was how widespread the sexual activity in that office was and the fact that it formed the basis for decisions on the terms and conditions of employment. Once the plaintiff declared herself a nonparticipant, her performance evaluations and the quality of her work assignments suffered.

While the court has made its holding on the hostile-environment theory, the Equal Employment Opportunity Commission takes the view that the facts of *Broderick* could also support a claim of quid pro quo harassment, since the managers' conduct sent a message to their female employees that job benefits would be awarded to those who participated in the office's sexual activity—that the way for women to get ahead was by engaging in sexual conduct.[7]

Employer Concerns and Responses

Since isolated instances of paramour preference are permissable, but widespread sexual activity creates a hostile-environment claim, even when the relationships involved are entirely consensual, the obvious question is, At what point does permissible preference become illegal conduct? Unfortunately, there are no easy answers. The way may become a little clearer, however, as cases advance through the courts, allowing them to analyze and interpret specific fact patterns in light of the 1990 statement by the commission. In the meantime, a prudent employer should consider these suggestions:

- Always bear in mind that sexual harassment allegations may involve more people and more issues than the obvious. Review and analyze the facts uncovered in your investigations in light of possible third-party claims as well as on the fundamental basis of harasser and harassee.
- Listen to corporate gossip, and follow up on frequent or repetitive rumors involving bosses and their subordi-

nates. Begin by examining personnel and production records, looking carefully at raises, promotions, assignments, and other reward opportunities. If a possible impropriety surfaces, speak in a straightforward way with the supervisor involved and caution him on the possible consequences of his behavior.

- Always focus on job-related rather than personal issues. Employers have a right to be concerned about what happens on their premises and to be informed enough to protect themselves against litigation risks. By focusing on the effects of even consensual relationships in the workplace, employers can achieve their objectives without prying into the private lives of either management or employees.
- Should the situation so warrant, structure a transfer opportunity for either party at the earliest possible time. Take care that the lower-level (and usually female) employee is not always the one requested to make the move, and that her options are fully reviewed with her.

NOTES

1. 29 CFR §1604.11 (1988).
2. 807 F. 2d 304 (2d Cir. 1986), cert denied, 108 S. Ct. 89, 98 L.Ed. 2d 50 (1987).
3. 262 Cal. Rptr. 842 (1989).
4. Fisher, note 3.
5. 570 F. Supp. 1197 (D. Del. 1983).
6. 685 F. Supp. 1269 (D.D.C. 1988).
7. EEOC Policy Guidance on Employer Liability for Sexual Favoritism, BNA's Daily Labor Report, February 15, 1990, pp. D1–3.

5

Conducting Sexual Harassment Investigations

Although technically, sexual harassment is a form of sex discrimination, as a cause of action it has come into its own, and a body of unique legal requirements and expectations has evolved. When allegations of sexual harassment are brought to an organization's attention, the employer has a clear legal duty to investigate those claims. The objective of that review is simple: to determine to the extent possible what happened, resolve the situation appropriately, and bring any illegal conduct to an end so that the workplace is once again free of any form of harassment.

Administrative agencies and courts have set out two key expectations for how that investigatory duty is to be discharged: promptly and thoroughly. For this purpose, a good rule of thumb for whether an investigation begins and ends promptly involves a matter of days, not weeks or months. In general, plan on beginning your investigation as soon as possible, but no more than two or three business days after the triggering event. Unless a set of circumstances is particularly complex, plan on concluding your investigation no more than ten business days later. This time frame may present some problems in geographically spread organizations, but it is expected that employers will demonstrate the seriousness of their concern for an harassment-free workplace, as well as for the well-being of the employees involved, by addressing sexual harassment situations quickly and effectively.

For an investigation to be conducted thoroughly, you must interview every individual who may have personal knowledge of the truth or falsity of the allegations themselves, or anyone who can shed significant light on the relationship between the accuser and the accused. This may include coworkers of the parties, individuals in physical proximity to their work stations, higher levels of management, or employees who may have relevant background information to offer. In addition, discussions with appropriate members of management and a close examination of corporate work records are usually most helpful, particularly when no witnesses are available.

The Importance of the Investigation

Minimizing Legal Liability

In the *Meritor* case, the Supreme Court listed several factors that tend to limit the liability of employers for the actions of their employees in sexual harassment cases, and urged courts and agencies to focus part of their inquiry on these factors. Included in the Court's listing was a clear policy statement prohibiting sexual harassment in the workplace, the seriousness of the employer's concern, and the imposition of significant corporate sanctions against individuals whose conduct breaches the employer's duty to provide an harassment-free work environment. The Court went on to identify the existence of internal complaint mechanisms that do not force complainants to bring their concerns to their immediate supervisors but that provide an alternative means for bringing sexual harassment concerns to the attention of management in a risk-free atmosphere. The complaint procedure, to be effective, needs to be communicated to employees; one of the better ways to disseminate that information is through the policy statement on sexual harassment (see Chapter 10).

Along with these preventive measures, the Court discussed the need for prompt and thorough investigation of all sexual harassment allegations, with effective and appropriate action taken as a result. Particularly in hostile-environment cases, an employer's legal liability can be greatly minimized, if not entirely eliminated, by prompt response to a sexual harassment allegation, effective investigation of the concern, and appropriate action taken to resolve the situation.

The Equal Employment Opportunity Commission is also prepared to provide employers who discharge their responsibilities in this area with an added incentive. Its 1988 policy guidance statement on sexual harassment ends:

> When an employer asserts it has taken remedial action, the Commission will investigate to determine whether the action was appropriate, and more important, effective. The EEOC investigator should, of course, conduct an independent investigation of the harassment claim and the Commission will reach its own conclusion as to whether the law has been violated. If the Commission finds that the harassment has been eliminated, all victims made whole, and preventive measures instituted, the Commission normally will administratively close the charge because of the employer's prompt remedial action.[1]

One of the most important things an employer can do, then, to lessen its legal liability, both administratively and judicially, is to conduct a proper investigation whose outcome provides an appropriate level of relief.

Such an investigation also enables the employer to review and understand all the significant facts and issues in each situation, assess the potential litigation exposures and potential costs, and feel reasonably confident that no "smoking gun" or legal bombshell is likely to be uncovered later. If employers also take the opportunity to learn the hard lessons that case-by-case investigation and analysis can teach them, the additional preventive steps that need to be taken can be identified and put into place, significantly decreasing the risks of similar future harassment activity.

Restoring Harmony to the Workplace

Aside from legal considerations, properly handled sexual harassment investigations also have considerable therapeutic employee-relations value:

- *For the accuser.* Satisfaction comes from having a complaint taken seriously and dealt with carefully and expeditiously. The resolution of the situation, even if not entirely to the complainant's liking, can provide a sense of closure and an opportunity to resume normal activities without contending with perceived or actual harassment.

- *For the accused.* A full and impartial review of management actions can clarify behavioral expectations and uncover festering subordinate concerns.

- *For observing employees in the department or unit.* Appropriate action will enhance the perception of the employer as concerned about the well-being of its employees, as open to discussions of employee concerns, and as willing to look into the facts and circumstances in a neutral, objective way and take action based on the findings. Over time, the trust employees feel in the organization to treat them fairly should increase, along with their satisfaction with the employer's complaint-resolution system. A pattern of fair and effective treatment will do more than any amount of rhetoric or public relations efforts to give the employer's internal complaint-resolution procedure an opportunity to settle employee concerns before they are brought to outside legal entities. The savings an employer achieves in decreased litigation expenses, as well as in stabilized productivity, can also be a significant contribution to the bottom line.

Who Should Investigate

Conducting sexual harassment investigations can require a special set of skills. To maximize the chances of success, the designated individual should be:

- Knowledgeable about the legal aspects of sexual harassment and the conflicting rights and responsibilities of all those involved.
- Experienced in handling general employee complaints, as well as other forms of discrimination claims.
- Familiar with the organization's structure, policies, practices, and management staff.
- Outside the involved parties' immediate chain of command—ideally in an ombudsman or service role.
- Credible to employees. The designated individual should enjoy a corporate reputation for straight shooting and independence.
- A trained facilitator, counselor, or someone who others find it easy to confide in.
- A friend or close associate of neither party.

If the complaint is within the organization's human resources department, or involves a friend or close associate of the individual designated to investigate the sexual harassment allegations, and thus neutrality and objectivity will be an issue, use outside counsel or an external consultant instead.

Whenever possible, employers should include both men and women in any group of designated investigators, giving complainants the ability to select a listener with whom they will feel the most comfortable.

The Issue of Confidentiality

Make Only Qualified Promises

Because of the inherent nature of sexual harassment allegations and the employer's duty to investigate them, organizations that promise absolute confidentiality to their complaining employees will not be able to keep their word. Policy statements, procedural documents, and oral communications should all be consistent in this issue, and should qualify the promise of confidentiality with appropriate words and explanations. Policy and procedural statements need to reference confidentiality in terms of "to the extent possible," "as much as possible," or "on a need-to-know basis." Interviewers and investigators need to fully explain why promises of absolute confidentiality cannot be given, as well as state what will be substituted: a pledge to limit discussion to only those individuals who must be contacted to fulfill the employer's legal duty to investigate and resolve.

The employer's position on this issue—its efforts to ensure that all matters uncovered in the course of the investigation will be carefully protected from overcommunication and the reasons for this approach—should be explained in some detail to everyone involved, including the parties themselves, other employees who need to be interviewed, and senior management.

Since the lack of confidentiality has serious potential employer and personal liability, should the reputation or good name of anyone involved in the matter be damaged, one of the critical functions of the designated investigator is to make sure that facts and opinions are discussed only with those persons who must be involved in the investigation itself, or in deciding its outcome. Even these individuals need to understand that discussing the matter with anyone other than the designated individual may have serious disciplinary consequences, as well as the potential for personal liability.

"Off-the-Record" Information

A related aspect of the confidentiality issue has to do with discussions held on informal, "off-the-record," or "in confidence only" bases. Human resources professionals in particular are frequently the recipients of sensitive information under these conditions. However, when the situation involves an allegation of sexual harassment there can be no such thing as an informal, "off-the-record," or "in confidence only" chat. Notice to the human resources professional, to a supervisor, or to any other member of management must be taken as notice to the employer that starts the promptness clock ticking and carries with it the duty to investigate.

This is true whether or not the individual disclosing the

information is herself a party to the conduct or wants an investigation to resolve the situation. Investigations must begin whether or not the complainant so desires (remember, she is not the only person with rights in this situation), and even whether or not she will cooperate to obtain all the facts.

To make sure there are no misunderstandings, the designated investigator needs to give a detailed explanation of the employer's position on confidentiality and the reasons for it. At the same time, the safeguards that have been put into place should be reviewed, and the importance of eliminating any harassing behavior should be stressed, so that employees are made to feel comfortable sharing the information the investigator needs to hear.

A Pledge of Nonretaliation

While absolute confidentiality cannot and should not be promised to anyone involved in the harassment investigation, a pledge of nonretaliation can and should be made. As with any other exercise of a legal right, employees should never be adversely affected by having brought an allegation of sexual harassment to management's attention, even if it later proves to be false. Not only is this an obvious requisite to a credible internal complaint-resolution system, it is a legal duty imposed by Title VII: Employees who, in good faith and belief, allege the existence of sexual harassment that later proves to be false may not be terminated or otherwise made to suffer for having done so. Only if malice, spite, or ill-will motivated the employee to make such an accusation may disciplinary action be considered.

Nonretaliation pledges should be a prominent part of any policy and procedural statements on the subject of sexual harassment.

Avoiding Defamation Claims

An Employer's Privilege and Its Risk

When sexual harassment is alleged, defamation is never very far away. Defamation is the publication to a third person of a false statement that tends to harm the reputation or good name of another. Since sexual harassment investigations almost always involve matters that might go to the heart of a person's reputation and good name, attention must be paid to minimizing the risks of defamation throughout the investigation and once it is concluded.

Employers do enjoy a qualified (not an absolute) privilege to do and say what is needed to conduct their business, but that privilege, although strong, can be lost. Discussing the situation with too many people, even only employees or management personnel, is a common way to lose the privilege. So is acting or appearing to act out of some malice or ill-will toward the employee claiming damages. Other ways to lose the privilege involve making statements believed to be truth but with no factual basis, and conveying information for no proper purpose. Whether as part of the investigatory process or later in giving potential employers or others reference information, it is critical to restrict the information that will be uncovered to only those few individuals in the workplace who must be told.

Safeguarding Corporate Documents

Investigators should hold all pertinent corporate records and other documents in a separate file, and should restrict access to those who have a legitimate need to see this information. The investigator can arrange for outside help, if needed, with typing or filing any documents created in the course of the investigation, rather than expose internal secretarial or clerical employees to their contents.

If, in the course of the investigation or at its conclusion, written documents are circulated to even a small number of individuals, the investigator should number the copies and distribute them with an attached instruction sheet prohibiting either copying or retention. Once read, the copies should be returned intact to the distributor.

Just the Facts, Please

Along with restricted access to information, the investigator should do everything possible to keep discussion focused on the facts. Because of the high emotions that usually accompany sexual harassment claims and the temptation to include extraneous information, supposition or simply innuendo can be very strong. You should encourage everyone involved, including senior management, to stick to the facts and avoid editorializing, characterization, or disparagement of the accused, his character, his job performance, or his family life.

As the individual with the most information about what has actually happened, be careful how and to whom you disclose what you know. The investigator's job is to gather the facts, not to spread the charges. To the extent possible, you should avoid phrasing questions with the accused's name. For example, instead of saying to a potential witness, "Did you see John touch Mary?" try, "Have you ever seen anyone touch Mary at work in a way that made her uncomfortable?" The broader question has the advantage of leaving the accused's name out of the matter while opening the door to a broader, perhaps expected response.

Dealing With Emotions

Sexual harassment investigations must, by their very nature, involve emotion-laden issues and touch deeply felt chords. The matters that must be discussed involve fundamental values and beliefs about sex—its proper role in life, views on the proper relationship at work between the sexes, what is and is not appropriate sexual conduct, and the relationship of sex in a person's overall value system. These are all highly personalized, intimate issues. The investigator must be empathetic enough to encourage complainants to talk about their situations frankly, yet professional enough to defuse emotions and avoid even the appearance of nonneutrality.

In addition to the hurdle that the very nature of discussion on sexual matters often presents are the very different perspectives of the parties when they are—as is the case most of the time—a man and a woman. The well-documented differences in how each sex views workplace interactions and responds to them have formed the basis for the recent change from a

"reasonable person" to a stricter "reasonable women" standard in three jurisdictions (see Chapter 3). Women as a group
tend to take sexual behavior much more seriously and to
characterize as sexual in nature more kinds of workplace behavior than do men.

As a result, the same set of facts and circumstances may
well receive two vastly different interpretations. A female employee may tend to say, "He leered at me; he propositioned
me; he fondled me." The male involved may characterize his
behavior as, "I smiled at her; I joked with her; I patted her on
the shoulder." It falls to the trained investigator, part blood-
hound, part counselor, part judge and jury, to interpret these
positions and bring the parties to a common understanding.

Planning the Investigation

Before beginning an investigation into allegations or incidents
of sexual harassment, always take the minimal amount of time
needed to carefully understand the objectives. Focus on the
key issues, and plan for how the needed results can best be
achieved. While every case will be different, taking the time to
plan will help make the process more uniform and more
effective:

 • Be sure the investigation plan being constructed meets
the employer's obligation to be both prompt and thorough.

 • Plan to begin with the complainant, or with the situation
if it arises other than through an employee's allegation.

 • Consider what records or other documents might be
helpful and where they can be found. Move as quickly as
possible to take possession or control of the records that are
most important to the case. Start a separate file for these
investigation documents, and include dated copies of all relevant policy, procedural, or handbook statements.

 • Set aside time to interview the accused, to touch base
with the next level of management, and to speak with third
parties. To be considered thorough, an investigation must

include every person who may be in a position to have first-hand knowledge of the alleged incident or of the circumstances involved.

▪ Include time to visit the physical area where the alleged harassment occurred. Note the size of the space, its proximity to other work stations, and the possible lines of sight available to potential witnesses.

▪ Construct the plan to meet the time frame suggested in this chapter for a prompt investigation. Create a sequenced list of who is to be interviewed, and fill in the actual dates and times of those meetings. Make sure to include any follow-up or monitoring sessions later required.

To conduct a proper investigation, you need to know what to focus on, what sexual harassment is and what it is not, and where these facts and circumstances fall on that continuum. Using the Equal Employment Opportunity Commission definition of sexual harassment as a yardstick, begin by comparing the facts and circumstances as you become aware of them, with the required elements contained in the agency's explanation (see Chapter 3). Note areas of possible congruence as well as those aspects of the case that differ from the key elements. Remember to pay particular attention to questions of supervisory actions, and notice whether or not conduct might have been welcomed. Keep this comparison up-to-date as the investigation progresses and as more facts and circumstances are disclosed.

Conducting the Investigation

No Claim Is Frivolous

To best protect the interests of the organization and all the parties involved, the investigator should treat every claim as both serious and sincere. Regardless of how frivolous, silly, or unusual an allegation may be, reserve judgment until the point when an informed decision can be made. Both line managers and human resources professionals are well acquainted with their populations and can probably recall instances when they believed that a given employee's concern was overblown, imaginary, or simply dead wrong. Regardless of an individual's tendency to bring concerns of this sort to management's attention, the assumption cannot be made that this is another of those times. Even the boy who cried wolf eventually did see one.

It's important to not taint the process with your own assumptions, stereotypes, or views of the parties involved. Simply because one employee has long service and one doesn't, or because one employee is an officer or a highly compensated manager and one isn't, or because one employee has demonstrated what the organization looks for in team effort or dedication, and one has not—none of these extraneous factors should have any bearing on whether sexual harassment actually took place. Your job is to determine as fully as possible what happened, and make an informed professional judgment about whether what happened constitutes sexual harassment.

All Parties Have Rights (and Obligations)

One of the reasons that sexual harassment is difficult to deal with is the problem of overlapping rights and obligations. All of those involved—the accuser, the accused, relevant third parties, company management, the human resources staff, the investigator, the organization itself—may have legal rights that conflict in the course of the investigation. A major goal of the investigation is to minimize these conflicts by dealing objectively with all concerned, handling situations quickly and completely, and minimizing possible damage to the reputation of each party.

The audience, however, is far broader than the small number of employees usually involved in an investigation. Even though every effort is made to limit the amount and type of information disseminated, the investigation itself will disrupt the workplace, and it will not be long before employees realize that something different—possibly involving a review by outsiders—is happening. Having ascertained at least that much (and possibly a good deal more), all employees in the organizational unit will look at (and judge) the company's responsiveness as well as its ability to restore harmony to the workplace. An organization that can deal quickly and appropriately with a sexual harassment allegation can also reap unexpected benefits in terms of increased employee trust and approval.

Notes and Reports

By all means, take notes during every interview, covering not only what is said but also emotions, gestures, or body language. Preserve these notes in their original handwritten state, complete with abbreviations, incomplete sentences, and disjointed phrases.

Written reports to the file or to management are a more complex matter. It will be difficult to predict, even possibly once the investigation is concluded, what fact or characterization might turn out to be the critical issue in a legal proceeding, and the report, like the notes, will be entirely discoverable (shown to the other side in any legal proceeding). The difference is that note-taking is a personal, idiosyncratic activity hard for others to interpret. Notes are at their best when used to jog the memory rather than stand on their own. The report, on the other hand, will be clearly typed, easy to interpret, and usually contain summaries of interviews and files that led to conclusory opinions and, ultimately, to recommendations for action. For all these reasons, it is wise to avoid writing a conclusory report and rely on oral briefings to management, letting the actions the organization takes in response speak for themselves.

If it becomes necessary to provide management with a written report, then do so only under the sponsorship of legal counsel, who can guide you on what can be done so that the report may be considered a privileged document unavailable to legal opponents.

Separate Allegations and Time Lines

If there is more than one set of allegations in a situation, separate each set and maintain that separation throughout the investigation. Not only will separating the allegations help keep the facts straight but it will make it much easier to determine whether sexual harassment has occurred in each instance based on its own merits, rather than on the combined effect of innuendo or deliberate smear tactics.

A time line for what happened, as the facts become available, helps set the events in the sequence in which they occurred. You can analyze this time line in terms of what was happening in the workplace at the same time, looking at the big picture for possible motivating factors or triggering events.

NOTES

1. Equal Employment Opportunity Commission, "Policy Guidance on Current Issues of Sexual Harassment," No. N-915.035 (October 25, 1988), p. 30.

6

Getting the Facts: Interviewing the Complainant

Most of the time, sexual harassment concerns or allegations of misconduct will come to the attention of the employer through an employee question or complaint. The logical place to start a discussion of investigative techniques, then, is with the fact-gathering phase: the interview with the complainant.

Explaining the Process

To avoid misunderstandings and possible later recriminations, every initial complainant interview should begin with a complete explanation of the investigatory process. Make sure to cover:

- The role of the investigator
- What will happen, and approximately when
- Who will decide the final outcome
- What the investigation will cover, including who else may be contacted and what records or documents may be used

This is also an ideal opportunity to let the complainant know that every effort will be made to limit discussion of the matters she is bringing to your attention to only those individuals who need to know the facts, and that it is expected she likewise will discuss her allegations only with you and with members of senior management or in-house counsel if that becomes desirable.

Assure the complainant that the company will make sure no retaliatory actions are taken because of her good-faith, sincere belief that she has been sexually harassed. Through open questions asking the complainant to put herself in the shoes of the individual she has named, make sure she understands that the allegations are serious, with the potential for serious damage to the individual's professional and personal reputations. For these reasons, and because the employer is responsible for providing a workplace free of harassment, her complaint or concern will be taken seriously and will be thoroughly reviewed. Explain that the facts will be gathered and assessed and the company will take what it decides is appropriate action based on them.

If the complainant is someone whose background might include culturally different ideas about touching others, the proper amount of physical space between individuals in the workplace, eye contact, or other aspects of physical relationships between relative strangers, now is a good time to learn what baseline assumptions or ideas play a part in her allegations of harassment. If cultural differences are major issues, it may be that one or two counseling sessions to help both parties understand and respect each other's ways may be all that is needed to resolve the misunderstanding. As in all matters where sexual harassment complaints or concerns are involved, take the time to fully explore and understand all the issues, rather than bring your own set of biases and assumptions to the table.

Use of Complaint Forms

Many individuals and corporations require individuals alleging sexual harassment to complete a written complaint form before any recognition is given to the claim. This is not a good policy.

A written document done at this time, before any interaction with the investigator has taken place, before any review of what legally constitutes sexual harassment, and before the process is fully explained may be quite different from the written explanation an individual might later produce. Yet it forms the starting point for the employer's response and is a key document in the event of later legal action.

Aside from these legal concerns, however, is a more fundamental reason for not requiring such a document to begin your investigative process: It may well have a distinct chilling effect on the environment and on the willingness of complainants to come forward and voice these concerns. A friendly, professional dialogue with a trained facilitator is one thing; a bureaucratic, impersonal form is quite another. Complaint forms can have a serious negative impact on the desire of individuals to bring sensitive issues to management for discussion. They also may present data in somewhat inaccurate, overblown, or overemotional terms. All in all, their use is strongly discouraged.

Learning What Happened

Let the complainant tell you in her own words what happened, once through, without interruption. Restate your understanding of what was said, and ask for agreement or correction until you have the basic facts defined to your satisfaction.

Then begin the process of adding flesh-and-blood detail to the bare bones of the facts. Probe for specifics at every opportunity, including the words that were said, the gestures that were made, where the touch was located on the body, the way the complainant was touched, and how the words interacted with the actions. This is no time for euphemisms or avoidance of frank language. If the complainant is too embarrassed to verbalize specifics, try to get the actions acted out while you verbalize for verification. Make sure you understand the level of emotion in the exchange—a calm tone of voice, shouts, screams, whispers?—and fully develop any possible triggering event or exchange. What was said or done by the complainant immediately prior to the harassing incident?

Look next to the details surrounding the event, including specific physical location, date, time of day, relationship to work routine, how the parties were dressed, whether the alleged harassment took place in the main area of the work-place or in a less-trafficked location, at an off-premises business function, during a meal or coffee break, and so on.

Explore the context of the behavior. Ask the employee if it could have been intended as a joke, whether similar actions had occurred in the past in a less serious vein, whether the harasser was surprised at her reaction. See Appendix A for specific interview questions.

Focus on Whether Conduct Was Welcomed

Carefully explore the parties' prior relationship. Find out how long they have known each other, whether they had a strictly business relationship or one that included meal or after-hours socializing alone or as part of a work group. Ask the complainant to describe the relationship she had with the alleged harasser before this incident, then ask her how she thinks he might respond to that question. Note the names of any other individuals who might be part of the work or social group and who are in a position to help you understand the relationship between the two parties.

Talk with the complainant about how the other person might have known that she was becoming uncomfortable with the complained-of behavior. Find out if she had indicated in any way, either through what she said or what she did, that the behavior was offensive to her. Discuss the frequency of the behavior, whether it had occurred in the past, and what her reactions had been to it then.

If it becomes clear in the course of the conversation that the complainant had participated in or had acquiesced to this behavior in the past, this needs to be fully developed, including dates and times of past actions to the extent the employee remembers them, what was said and done at those times by the complainant and by the individual she is accusing of misconduct, and most important, what has happened since to make the behavior unwelcome. Look for a possible escalation in the type of behavior itself (more coarse verbalizations, more intimate touchings, more risqué displays), or some change in the relationship between the parties that made the complainant unwilling to participate in or to acquiesce to the same level of behavior.

If it becomes apparent that the parties had a dating or even an intimate relationship in the past, it is critical how the other individual would have come to know that previous behavior was now no longer welcome. Particularly when consensual relationships go sour, or one party to the affair wants to end it but the other cannot, mutual counseling and sound preventive measures may resolve the matter informally to the satisfaction of both individuals.

Focus on the Issue of Notice

When the Supervisor Is the Claimed Harasser

The employer is responsible for the actions of those whom he has entrusted with power over others in his behalf, and the employer's policies and practices are the vehicles to effect the required loss of tangible job benefits in quid pro quo cases. By reviewing his own records, the employer could have known and therefore should have known of the situation and addressed it.

If the individual in the complaint is the supervisor, focus on the effects of the harassing behavior on the complainant in the workplace. Find out whether she believes that job raises, promotions, assignments, and other job benefits have been handled fairly, or if she believes that she (and perhaps others) has been singled out for ill treatment because of her reactions to the sexual behavior. If the complainant has worked for that individual for some time, try to pinpoint the time period when the complainant's dissatisfaction began with the terms and conditions of her employment. Find out whether performance reviews have been done, what ratings the complainant received, and what reasons were given to her for those ratings.

Similarly, if the complainant indicates that raises or promotions have been withheld, find out what explanations, if any, were given to her, and whether they lend themselves to verification through file records.

If there is a significant gap between the time of the alleged incidents and this complaint, ask about what led to the decision to come forward at this particular time. Look for workplace events or decisions that might have triggered the complaint at this time, or that might shed some light on the complainant's motivation in light of the time gap.

When the Alleged Harasser Is a Coworker

The focus needs to be on the level of knowledge the particular supervisor might have had about the alleged harassing activity, including how it might have come to his attention, whether he ever participated with the coworker in the harassing activity, and, of course, what he did when he learned of the situation. Look for whether the supervisor, if asked for help by the complainant, acknowledged the seriousness of the offense and made any effort to stop it. If so, find out what he did and why it proved to be ineffective. Ask whether, to her knowledge, the coworker was ever disciplined for the behavior in any way.

When the Alleged Harassers Are a Group

When sexual harassment situations involve more than one coworker's participation, always carefully separate the allegations involving each member of the group, and make sure these continue to be treated as distinct, separate incidents so that they can ultimately be judged on their own merit and the complaints against each individual can be effectively answered. At the same time, be aware of the cumulative effect of the group activity on the complainant, and treat it as a separate entity as well.

When the Alleged Harasser Is an Outsider

Occasionally, the individual accused of sexual misconduct is an outsider—a visitor, customer, salesperson, or other guest in the workplace. Find out whether any company supervisor or employee was aware of the harassing activity, how that might have been brought to someone's attention, and whether any efforts were made to stop it from occurring again.

Looking for Existing Patterns

Sexual harassment is usually not an isolated occurrence, but rather one incident in a pattern of sexually oriented behavior or misconduct. While the opportunity presents itself, explore the possibilities of patterns on the parts of both parties.

Discuss whether this has ever happened to the complainant in the past in this organization, particularly with this alleged harasser. If past incidents surface, find out whether they were brought to the attention of management and, if not, why not. Ask the complainant if she is aware of anyone else in the work group, past or present, who might have had similar difficulties with the alleged harasser.

Use of Internal Procedures

The Equal Employment Opportunity Commission and many courts believe that a complainant is entitled to think that sexual harassment will be condoned by an organization if it does not establish the preventive measures of clear, prohibitive policy statements and effective procedural steps. However, the existence of these tools, which are designed to provide the employer notice and an opportunity to act, tends to disadvantage a complainant who fails to use them. The use of an internal complaint-resolution system in a timely way, rather than significantly after the fact, can boost a complainant's credibility considerably.

The converse is true as well: Complainants who ignore the

employer's sincere efforts to uncover and resolve sexual harassment situations do so at their peril. The Equal Employment Opportunity Commission, for example, takes the position that employees who know their employers have provided an internal complaint-resolution system in these situations but fail to use it will not later be able to successfully claim constructive discharge because of sexual harassment activity.

Constructive discharge occurs when the employee is not actually dismissed but feels compelled to resign. Without the job loss constructive discharge permits, complainants might be unable to bring any claim of sexual harassment at all, but clearly not a quid pro quo claim, where the employer's self-help is a good deal less effective in reducing possible liability. The possibility of having the state agency or the Equal Employment Opportunity Commission add a claim of quid pro quo harassment to one of hostile-environment harassment is also eliminated if the complainant fails to use the internal complaint-resolution mechanism while alleging constructive discharge.

If complainants have failed to use the internal complaint-resolution system, and have waited a significant time to voice the complaint, it is important to find out why, in terms of both the outcome of this particular investigation and also as a method of improving the company's mechanism for effectively dealing with sensitive issues in a timely way.

Corroborating Witnesses

Always ask the complainant whether anyone witnessed any of the behavior she describes, whether seeing it as it happened, hearing the complainant and the accused individual exchanging words, or learning about it from the complainant after the fact.

This last question, if answered in the affirmative, can be helpful and present difficulties at the same time. It is always helpful to have someone available who has been told of misconduct at the time it occurred. This acts as an enhancement to the complainant's credibility and makes the person a possible corroborating witness. However, the fact that the plaintiff has told at least one and possibly a number of coworkers about the harassment raises both defamation issues and employee-relations concerns.

Begin by reiterating your request that the complainant not share any further information with anyone other than those individuals already identified. Remind the complainant that these are serious allegations and that, true, false, or inconclusive, they can do serious harm to the accused's reputation at work and in the community.

Make a listing of all witnesses identified by the complainant and the specific behaviors they may have seen, with approximate time frames. At the same time, take the opportunity to learn a little about the relationships the complainant has with each named witness—close friend, relative, long-time associate, short-term acquaintance, and so on.

When there are no corroborating witnesses, of course it does not mean that the harassment incidents did not occur. In fact, most of the time sexual harassment tends to happen in situations where the two parties are alone and uninterrupted. That does not make the harassment charge less real. When there are no corroborating witnesses, however, your examination of other corroborating evidence becomes all the more important.

Other Corroborating Evidence

Once you learn the exact nature of the complainant's allegations, begin immediately to identify the organizational records, documents, reports, and other materials that might be used to corroborate all or part of what she claims. Some of the items to consider include:

- Complainant's personnel file
- Accused individual's personnel file
- Quantity and quality production records
- Performance reviews

- Annual salary budget projections, forced rankings, or salary justification memos
- Annual bonus projections, assessments of achievements against goals, or other award criteria, if any
- Department or unit promotional records, indicating open positions, dates, and how they were filled
- Any records of job bids or postings for the open positions you find, including whether or not the complainant applied, and was interviewed, or whether the job was excluded from bid
- Any disciplinary warnings or negative notes from the accused, if the supervisor, to complainant
- Records of any similar allegations the complainant has raised in the past, particularly with respect to the same individual
- Records of special assignments, training opportunities, and other "soft" job benefits controlled by the alleged harasser.

All of these, together with other relevant documents that may shed some light on the situation, need to be carefully reviewed. Significant events should be placed on the time line begun earlier, and viewed in light of the dates and times that the complainant has specified in terms of both the harassing behavior and the overall relationship between the complainant and the accused.

When supervisors and tangible job benefits are involved, these corporate documents need to be examined for both internal consistency and consistency with the complainant's allegations. Examine performance documents to see if the same rating factors were used for the same job functions; if backup documentation exists for any lower-than-average rating categories; or if raise, bonus, and promotion opportunities provided were consistent with that level of performance. Examine the management rationale for particular actions and the application of corporate policy and practice to note any results that may at first glance seem unusual or arbitrary.

Look for any available nonjudgmental trackings of performance, such as computer-system measures of quantity, customer or other nonsupervisory commendations or thank-you notes, quality audit results or percentage of work that needed to be returned—in short, look for every objective source and every reasonable indicator of actual performance and supervisory rating.

If discrepancies between these two assessments are extreme, note the issue, date, and document for later review with the supervisor involved.

If favoritism is alleged, the same review ought to be done with respect to the individual the supervisor is said to favor. If the tangible job benefits awarded seem unwarranted by documentation or objective criteria, add these to your list of discussion topics. Should the situation call for it, review the documentation on each member of the department or unit, and see what patterns emerge.

The Issue of Self-Help

Sometimes sexual harassment situations can be resolved fairly easily simply by confronting the harasser with a demand to stop the offensive behavior. Such self-help can be useful when:

- Taking the initiative would help the complainant feel less victimized and more in control of the situation. Many commentators have noted that one of the worst results of sexual harassment in the workplace is a loss of self-esteem and empowerment. By allowing a complainant to take self-help measures before the investigation proceeds any further, you may be able to accomplish some of your own objectives (such as ending the offensive behavior) while helping the harassed employee feel much less like a victim.

- Complainants who had once welcomed particular behaviors but no longer welcome them may not have communicated that change to the other party. In this case, a self-help remedy provides the notice to the other individual and may be enough action to stop the offensive behavior.

- Complainants might prefer a much less formal resolution.

Make sure that the complainant understands that, regardless of the success or failure of her self-help effort, the investigation once started must continue to its end, although the scope might be modified. Complainants must agree to try their self-help remedy as soon as possible, and to let you know what happens. On behalf of the employer, however, be sure you reserve the organization's right to warn, discipline, or take other action appropriate to the situation once the investigation is concluded, regardless of the success of the complainant's self-help remedy. Complainants may need to be reminded that they are not the only party with rights and obligations in the situation.

What Does the Complainant Want?

End the interview with a key question. Ask the complainant what she would like to see done, what action she would like the employer to take, what she would like to see happen to the accused. The response to this can be very telling, in terms of both the complainant's expectations of the investigative process and her reasonableness and credibility.

If expectations that are not likely to be met come to the surface, now is the time to dispel these notions and replace them with an explanation of the process and its possible outcomes.

If complainant's response to the question of what she would like to see happen to the alleged harasser is vindictive, vengeful, or malicious—such as "I want him fired!" "I want to make sure his wife and children know about this!" "I want to make sure he never works anywhere ever again!"—and particularly if this reaction seems extreme in light of the specific events or circumstances, note the response for further consideration of motive and believability.

Credible complainants respond in ways appropriate to the situation, so that the preferred action bears a strong relationship to the level of harassment discussed—or, in simple terms, so that the punishment fits the crime. They understand that there are frequently two or more sides to a story, and that the employer is in a difficult situation.

Updating the Definition Comparison

Once the complainant provides a more detailed rendition of the facts and circumstances from her perspective, use this new information to update your comparison of this case and its characteristics with the general definition of sexual harassment used by the Equal Employment Opportunity Commission.

If it becomes clear early on that the facts and circumstances do not rise to a legal level of sexual harassment, discuss this with the complainant, assuring her that the organization will respond appropriately to the behavior and work with the individual to make sure he modifies his actions to conform to what is expected behavior in a business setting. Explain the "shuttle diplomacy" approach you expect to take, and that you are hopeful of resolving the matter to everyone's satisfaction.

Assessing Complainant Credibility

Along with clarifying the facts and circumstances, your mission is to assess the credibility of the complainant. Base your impressions on the internal consistency of her story; what she presents as her motivations, what corroboration is available, and the body language and voice inflections you observe while she speaks. While you will have a number of later opportunities to add to your impression, and will make a judgment only after all the facts are in, take a moment to note your first impressions from the initial meeting.

Offering Interim Relief

Based on the facts and circumstances, and your assessment of the complainant, you may want to provide some form of immediate relief until the investigation is concluded. This should be considered when:

- The complainant is in a highly emotional state.
- The relationship between the complainant and the alleged harasser has become so adversarial that peace in the workplace has been disrupted for everyone, and going to work has become a highly unpleasant chore for the complainant.
- The allegations are very serious and very believable.
- The complainant requests some measure of relief.

Consider offering temporary transfer to a position using the same general skills, with retention of all compensation and benefit levels; a paid leave of absence until the investigation is concluded; an unpaid leave of absence until the investigation is finished; or reassignment to a different building, floor, or department, or a special project that can be completed either at home or in a different work area. Let the complainant help select the best option for management's review and immediate decision.

Removing the complainant from the harassing environment clearly indicates the seriousness with which management takes the allegations and relieves not only the woman involved but observing coworkers as well.

If the Complainant Also Files a Charge

If, during the initial discussion, you learn that the complainant has also filed an administrative charge, that knowledge must not result in a misguided decision to curtail or shut down the investigation entirely, pending the outcome of the state or Equal Employment Opportunity Commission charge. Indeed, the commission has filed suit when employers have terminated their investigation in the face of an administrative charge, calling the termination an unlawful retaliatory measure in violation of Section 704(a) of Title VII.

As long as the complainant is willing to cooperate in the

internal investigation, the benefits of a proper review and response remain. Indeed, with or without the complainant, it will be necessary to thoroughly investigate and respond to the charge once it is served. Alert your counsel that a formal charge has been filed, but that the investigation will continue.

Preparing a Signed Statement

While there are sound reasons to forgo a written complaint form as a prerequisite to management action, it can be beneficial to work with the complainant to prepare a statement of her position that she then signs and that goes into the case file.

Let the complainant know that her statement may be shown to members of senior management, to legal counsel, to any government agency personnel that may become involved, and to other individuals who may be interviewed during the investigation, including the accused. Its accuracy is therefore most important. While drafting the statement together can add clarity and detail to the summary of the allegations, make sure the complainant carefully reads and reviews the statement and that she agrees that it represents a fair and accurate account of what she has said to you. Ask her to sign the statement once its language has been finalized and it has been typed and read over. The original goes into the case file, with copies to the complainant and the investigator.

If the complainant seems reluctant to work with you to draft a position statement, offer her a quiet room and as much time as is necessary for her to draft her own version. Review the language in her document carefully to make sure it accurately recounts what she has said to you. Have it typed and reread, and ask the complainant to sign her name. Distribute the document in the same way: the original in the case file, copies to the complainant and the investigator.

If the complainant refuses to sign anyone's account of her statement, remind her that unsubstantiated allegations have serious consequences, including the possibility for personal liability. Probe to see if there is a reasonable explanation for her unwillingness. If not, draft the position paper yourself, carefully noting her refusal to sign, and characterize the statement as your best understanding of her position, based on your conversation.

7

Meeting With the Accused

Once you have interviewed the complainant, examined the documentary evidence, and given some thought as to how you will approach the accused, you're ready to meet with him. This chapter tells you how to conduct such a meeting. For sample interview questions, see Appendix A.

When the Supervisor Is the Accused

Presenting the Allegation

Begin your meeting with a supervisor accused of sexual harassment by letting him know that a serious matter has been raised, that he has been connected to it, and that it involves unwelcome behavior on his part. Avoid characterizing the behavior as sexual harassment, and avoid talking about the matter in terms of a "charge," "lawsuit," "allegation" or "claim." Instead, talk about the facts that have been brought to your attention or the situation that needs to be clarified and resolved.

Explaining the Process

As with the complainant, take the time needed to review:

- The employer's obligations under the law

- Your role as the investigator
- What will happen and approximately when
- Who will decide the final outcome
- What the investigation will cover
- The seriousness of the matter and that every effort will be made to conduct a neutral, objective, and professional review
- The ultimate objectives of the investigation: not to determine the truth and assign blame but to end the illegal or inappropriate activity, if there is any, and take preventive measures to see that it does not recur

Make sure the supervisor understands that he has both a management and a personal stake in cooperating fully. As a member of the management team, he is responsible for implementing the employer's policy in this area, and for the climate and morale in his unit. As an individual, he has a need to see that all the facts and circumstances are uncovered so that the matter will be fully explored rather than left to be grist in the corporation's rumor mill.

Identifying the Complainant

Should the accuser be identified? There are two schools of thought about disclosing the name of the complainant. The nondisclosure proponents are concerned about the complainant's emotions and the sensitive nature of the claim, as well as the practical possibility of retaliatory actions. Those in favor of disclosure cite the common-law tradition requiring individuals accused of a crime to know who is making the charge. Add to this the obstacles to a thorough and effective investigation created when trying to keep the complainant's name secret. As a practical matter, it becomes quite difficult to discuss specific facts and issues without indirectly giving the accused enough information to determine who has made the allegation. Naming the individual also eliminates the appearance of nonneutrality, and puts the parties on a more equal footing for the investigation. For all of these reasons, prompt disclosure of the name of the complainant is highly recommended.

Reviewing the Facts

Present a brief summary of the facts calmly but without apology, and note the supervisor's response. The most common responses include anger, surprise, flat denial, or defensive statements of hurt and betrayal. Carefully observe and note the response and the body language that went with it.

When the initial reaction has subsided, ask the supervisor what he believed happened during the incidents the complainant has cited. Allow him to relate his understanding of the situation through once, then return to it for specific, step-by-step review. As with the complainant, make sure the discussion is specific and detailed enough to provide the information you need to make an informed judgment later on. Note dates, times, places, circumstances, dress, words exchanged, as well as the specifics of the alleged acts.

If you were able to obtain a signed statement from the complainant, show that to the supervisor and give him an opportunity to read it through. If no such statement was signed, recite the facts of the situation as related to you by the complainant, providing specific details as you go along. Begin going through the facts, step by step, noting areas of agreement, disagreement, or where corroboration by third parties might be possible.

Once the details of the supervisor's perspective have been fleshed out, turn to a discussion of their context. Talk about the overall climate and norms in the unit, the level of sexual language and joking, and what part the supervisor plays in those office conversations. If touching is an issue, find out how the supervisor characterizes those contacts and in what possible business context he places them.

Focusing on Whether the Conduct Was Welcome

Begin your inquiry by asking the supervisor to describe his relationship with the complainant, noting whether the description is entirely work related, entirely personal, or a mix of the two. Find out how long the parties have known each other, and on what basis.

Ask the supervisor whether he had noticed any recent changes in the complainant's behavior toward him, or reactions that might indicate in any way, orally or through body language, that the behavior in question was offensive to her. Find out how frequently the behavior occurred in the past, and what the complainant's reactions to it had been at that time.

If the supervisor's response indicates that his behavior was welcomed at some time in the past, make sure you clearly note what that time period was and what specific behaviors occurred on each of those occasions, to the best of his recollection. If the complainant actively participated in sexual joking or hung a male nude in her cubicle or discussed her sex life in a frank and open way—if the complainant did or said anything that might indicate that sexuality was a welcome topic—ask for specifics with time frames. See if there was an escalation of the behavior, a sudden lack of participation by the complainant, or a change in the relationship between the parties that might be a factor in the complainant's change in behavior.

If the parties had a dating or an intimate relationship in the past, note the time frame and explore whether the complainant did or said anything to the supervisor to indicate a change in her feelings and, if so, what that indicator was. Be aware that paramour preference may become a third-party issue for at least the period of that relationship (see Chapter 4). Make a mental note to examine the documentary evidence with this concern in mind—indicators of favoritism may be present as well as possible indicators of harassment.

When Coworkers Are the Accused

Getting Background Information

When the situation involves a coworker or a group of coworkers rather than a supervisor, it's still a good idea to start with the immediate supervisor of the accused if the complainant and coworker work for the same person, or with the supervisors of both parties together.

Briefly give the supervisor the minimal facts of the sexual

harassment allegation: who the parties are and what the offensive behavior entails. Ask for whatever information the supervisor may have, whether official or informal, concerning:

- The nature of the parties' relationship
- How long they've worked together
- Whether they've known each other before
- Whether they socialize alone or as a group
- Whether they eat lunch or take breaks together
- Whether they are closely involved in each other's work or independent of each other's job functions
- Whether the supervisor has observed anything that would lead him to believe the alleged behavior occurred or that it was unlikely to have occurred
- Whether the complainant might have a work-related or personal motive for bringing a claim of sexual harassment against this particular individual
- Whether there have been any unusual incidents or other allegations raised by either party against the other

Focusing on Notice

When coworkers are accused of sexual harassment, a central point of inquiry has to be whether or not the supervisor had any knowledge of the matter and, if so, what he elected to do about it. Find out if the supervisor observed any inappropriate language, displays, or jokes in the work group; any reactions of discomfort or embarrassment; or any levels of touching that could have been considered offensive. Find out if the supervisor was told by anyone directly, or had picked up rumblings of possible misconduct involving these two parties.

If any possibility of notice exists, find out if the supervisor took any action as a result and, if so, what he did, when he did it, and with what result.

Caution the supervisor about discussing the situation with others, including the individuals involved most directly. Briefly explain your role and your expectations for how the investigation will proceed, and let him know that you will brief him at the conclusion of the review. If there will be disciplinary consequences, he may be involved in implementing them.

Presenting the Allegation

With the added benefit of supervisory background information, meet with the named coworker and briefly advise him of why you're there. (If more than one individual is named, meet with each person separately, dealing only with the allegations specifically concerning each). Meet in a neutral space, if possible, such as a conference room, but one sufficiently removed from the work area so that remaining employees will not see a parade of associates heading toward the interview room.

Present a summary of the facts to the individual and note the response, both oral and otherwise. When the initial reaction has subsided, ask the accused what he believes happened during the incident cited. Ask for his side of the story and let him tell it through once without interruption. When you have the initial rendition, go over it again, filling in specifics and details to the extent possible. Note dates, times, places, circumstances, dress, words exchanged, as well as the specifics of what is claimed to have happened.

If you have a signed complainant statement, show it to the individual and give him an opportunity to read it through. If the complainant refused to sign such a statement, recite the facts of the situation, as related to you, in some detail. Compare the coworker's version with the complainant's version, noting areas of agreement, disagreement, or possible third-party corroboration.

Once the details have been filled in, ask the coworker to explain the context of the behavior. Find out if this is typical of the climate in that department or unit—the level of sexual language and joking—and what part the complainant may have played in those conversations or activities. If touching is an issue, find out how the coworker characterizes those contacts and whether he was aware that they caused offense.

Again focusing on the issue of notice, find out whether the supervisor was aware of these activities, whether he participated in them, and whether he had made any attempt to stop them in the past.

Explaining the Process

Make sure the coworker understands what the process will involve and how it will work:

- That a complete investigation is required by law
- What the investigation will cover and who will conduct it
- What the likely time frame is for concluding the investigation and who will decide the final outcomes
- That the matter is serious, and for that reason every effort will be made to conduct a neutral, objective, and professional review
- What the objectives of the investigation are

Focusing on Whether the Conduct Was Unwelcome

Ask the coworker to describe his relationship with the complainant, and whether the complainant's behavior changed during that time. Follow the same line of inquiry as for supervisory accused, probing for signs of past welcomeness or clear indications that the behavior was no longer welcome.

When the Accused Is an Outsider

In the event that the alleged harasser is an outsider—a customer, a vendor, a visitor, a service person—meet with the complainant's supervisor to inform him of the allegation and ask him what he may himself know with respect to the parties involved and the situation. Once you've briefly given the supervisor the factual highlights, focus on whether he was aware of any misconduct, whether the complainant brought it to his attention, and what, if anything, he did as a result. Make sure you note the relevant time frames, as well as the names of any potential corroborating witnesses.

Corroborating Witnesses

Ask the accused, whether a coworker or a supervisor, whether anyone witnessed any of the behavior described, or if anyone was in a position to see or hear anything of the parties' relationship.

Make a list of all potential witnesses identified, along with the specific behaviors they may have seen or heard, and their time frames. Find out a little about the relationship the accused has with each potential witness, including type and duration.

Other Corroborating Evidence

When the accused is the supervisor, a good deal of corporate documentation of the relationship probably exists and is known to you. At this time, however, make certain that any additional documentary evidence the supervisor may have, including his desk file on the complainant and other relevant individuals, is identified and properly stored with other investigatory files.

On the basis of your review of the corporate records, begin exploring the supervisor's business rationale for each significant raise, promotion, ratings, or other job benefit decision made concerning the complainant. Check whether these are well documented, internally consistent, and in line with organizational policy and practice. Particularly note whether required levels of authorization for personnel actions have been followed. If the complainant's file indicates sudden shifts in ratings, rankings, or other indicators of performance, find out what happened to cause these differences and how they were documented.

Assessing the Accused's Credibility

As with the complainant, ask the accused what he is prepared to do about the situation and what suggestions he might have about how this matter can best be resolved. Add his response to your overall impressions of credibility, noting them while they're still fresh in your mind. Base your impressions on the internal consistency of the story, available corroboration, and body language and voice inflections observed during your interview.

Updating the Definition Comparison

Once the accused has had an opportunity to provide a detailed rendition of the facts and circumstances from his perspective, use this new information to update your comparison of the facts of the case with the Equal Employment Opportunity Commission definition of sexual harassment.

Since you have now taken detailed information from both the complainant and the accused, compare information, noting areas of similarity and significant discrepancy for possible follow-up interviews.

Language and Labels

How you talk about the allegations, the language you select to characterize or describe the behavior that is cited, can be a critical element in the success or failure of the resolution effort. Using harsh language with an individual accused of sexual misconduct can only serve to heighten his defensiveness and raise the investigative stakes, making it more difficult to bring the parties to a satisfactory conclusion.

For instance, labeling an individual as a "sexual harasser" is a very strong statement that is seldom entirely supported by the facts. It is a rare case that is so clearly black and white; the usual situation is a shade of gray. Not only is labeling unnecessary, it heightens tensions in the workplace, creates a stigma for the accused individual, whether he is ultimately cleared or not, and is therefore counterproductive. Likewise, feeding the accused's anger at the injustice and inappropriateness of the label allows the accused to see himself as a victim, thus avoiding any focus on the inappropriate behavior that began it all.

The potential effects of loose language on an accused individual's career, family life, and community standing can be devastating. It can also, of course, result in a suit for common-law defamation—damage to the reputation through a false published assertion—that will be very difficult to refute.

Always take care with the language you use, whether dealing with the complainant, the accused, corroborating witnesses, senior management, or, of course, legal representatives, including investigators from the Equal Employment Opportunity Commission. Use language that is fair, that does not minimize the behavior but does not sensationalize it, either. Talk about "a serious matter," "a sensitive issue," and behavior that might be called "inappropriate," rather than leaping to conclusions of "sexual harassment," "sexual abuse," or "corporate rape." Even once the facts are in and the judgment must be made, avoid labels that can only serve to increase litigation and decrease the chances for a successful resolution.

Preparing Signed Statements

Ask each individual you interview to help you draft a clear, detailed summary of his or her position, making sure that the accused person reads his statement and agrees that it is a fair and accurate representation of what he has said to you. Ask him to sign the statement once you've agreed on the language, and it has been typed up and read over. Place the original in the case file, with copies to the accused and the investigator.

If the accused is reluctant to help you draft a position statement, offer him the time and private space to draft a statement of his own. Review his language carefully to make sure it reflects what you've been told, then have the statement typed and re-read, and ask the accused to sign his name. Distribute the document in the same way: the original in the case file, copies to the accused and yourself.

If the accused refuses to sign such a statement, draft one yourself, carefully noting the refusal to sign and characterizing the statement as your best understanding of the position, based on your conversation.

8

Meeting With Relevant Others

For purposes of this type of investigation, consider any individual who might have firsthand knowledge of the situation, or firsthand knowledge of the relationship of the parties, to be a *relevant other*. That may include workers in the same department or unit, those in a physically adjacent department with good lines of sight, the management level above the immediate supervisor, staff personnel involved in prior matters concerning the parties, or anyone whose name was mentioned in the course of the interviews with either the complainant or the accused.

Should the complainant lodge a complaint with a state agency or the Equal Employment Opportunity Commission, it's likely that the administrative investigator will also interview the complainant's counselor, physician, therapist, or other outside individual she may have informed or consulted. The employer, however, does well to confine the company's investigation to individuals in the workplace.

Explaining the Process

Since most individuals to be interviewed are likely to be non-supervisory employees and, human nature being what it is, are aware of something going on and are curious to know the details, it is important to begin your interview with a thorough review of the process and the organization's expectation for the individual's participation. Make sure you cover:

- The employer's legal obligation to investigate all matters raised.
- The difference between this undertaking and a trial in a court of law. Here, everyone has rights and obligations, some of which may conflict, but guilt or innocence is not the issue and will likely not be ascertained. The issue is the employer's obligation to establish and maintain a workplace free of harassment, and to take whatever steps are necessary to do so.
- That the investigation will be conducted in a neutral, objective, and professional way, and that it will focus on facts rather than gossip, innuendo, or rumor.
- That as the investigator, you will be asking them for personal knowledge or background information. Make sure the individuals understand the difference between personal knowledge and hearsay or other indirect accretion of information, and the difference between fact and opinion.
- Who will decide the final outcome, and that the result will be focused on making sure all behavior in the department or unit is appropriate for a place of business and not offensive to others.
- That sexual harassment is not "in the eye of the beholder," but that it has a specific legal definition and a set of tests for determining whether it has occurred. Make sure each individual understands that terms such as "sexual harassment" are frequently used cavalierly, but that in the workplace there are a number of behaviors that may be inappropriate to the surroundings yet not rise to a legal level of harassment.
- That such a matter has been raised, and the individual may have been in a position to witness, observe, or hear something that could help us determine what actually happened.

Phrasing Your Questions

Remember that, as the individual with the most knowledge of the situation, you are in a unique position. It is not difficult to inadvertently reveal information or otherwise spread the facts of the situation around the workplace. Before meeting with each individual, check your notes from past interviews and from your file reviews to see what specific areas you need to cover with each person. Then spend a few minutes carefully constructing your questions to minimize the information you give, and consequently the opportunity for possible later defamation concerns.

Begin each conversation with the statement that the complainant has brought a serious matter to management's attention that involves sexually inappropriate behavior in the workplace. Ask the basic question of whether this witness has ever personally observed, witnessed, or heard anything that would indicate the complainant was being made uncomfortable at work, or that she found her work environment offensive. With luck, you may receive a relevant response that assists you in bringing the situation to a close.

If not, move to the next level of question and ask directly about the relationship between the complainant and the individual she has accused of misconduct. While the employer's qualified privilege will protect against liability when using the names of individuals involved as long as the use is not reckless or malicious, the better practice is to start by revealing the least amount of information, and proceed from there. Carefully note the response, probing for details of dates, times, places, situation, dress, what was seen or heard, exactly when the problem surfaced, what the complainant's reaction was, who else might have relevant information. See Appendix A for sample interview questions.

Focusing on the Facts

If a witness indicates that the complainant told him or her directly about the situation, either at the time it allegedly occurred or later, find out exactly what was said and when the conversation took place, to the witness's best recollection. Not only will this provide information on concurrent statements but it will also indicate if there has been a breach of the prohibition against discussion of the situation with anyone but the investigator. If a breach has occurred, consider issuing a written warning to the complainant so she knows the organization is serious about preserving the fullest possible extent of confidentiality, and that disciplinary consequences will occur if discussion continues.

Witnesses responding to your initial, broad-based inquiry may, in fact, give information not about the individual the complainant has named but about others in the workplace. Should that occur, note the information, probe for details of time, date, place, situation, and what specifically was heard or seen. If warranted, return later to the complainant and ask about the recounted incident. Find out if this was an unreported prior situation, welcomed behavior that was not offensive to her, or an additional piece of the puzzle.

Focusing on the Parties' Relationship

To learn more about the parties' past and present relationship, again begin with a broad-based question, such as asking whom in the work group the complainant usually socialized with, had coffee or lunch with, went out after work with, or dated. To complete the general picture, go on to ask whom in the work group the complainant had a strictly business relationship with. Witnesses may not immediately think of the complainant's supervisor as a member of the work group, so you may have to specifically ask if the comments include the complainant's supervisor.

If no relevant information surfaces, go to the next level of questioning, naming the individual involved and specifically asking about current and past relationships, reminding each witness of the need to speak only from personal knowledge. Note the details of the response, probing for specific dates, times, places, situations, exactly what was seen or heard, and what complainant's reactions seemed to be.

Warning Witnesses About Further Discussion

It is particularly important that the interviewees understand the need for no discussion of the sensitive matter other than with the investigator. First, corroborating witnesses and relevant others probably account for the largest number of individuals involved in the investigation, and most of them are from one area of the organization and therefore know each other fairly well. Because of these factors, and because they are involved only peripherally, the temptation to discuss the situation among themselves is a strong one.

In addition, if supervisory misconduct has been alleged, these witnesses are likely to be subordinates of the same individual. If care is not taken in how the investigator speaks of the supervisor, or if the objectives and limitations of the investigation are not fully explained, the supervisor may have to live with subordinates who now view him with ridicule or contempt. In your dealings with relevant others, then, never say or do anything that implies lessened respect for the supervisor, or be careless or loose in the language you use to describe the allegations. Not all allegations are accurately presented by complainants, and not all situations are cut-and-dried. But when supervisors and subordinates are involved, the potential for damage to someone's reputation is high; preventive action should be taken before the situation deteriorates.

Make sure each interviewee understands that discussion of any aspect of the situation with other employees or outside of the workplace (particularly in small communities, where what is said has a way of coming back to the individuals involved) is not permitted, and that disciplinary sanctions, up to and including termination, can and will be imposed for disregarding this prohibition.

Assessing Witness Credibility

After listening to each witness and noting the individual's presentation of facts from his or her unique perspective as well as each person's facial expression, voice, and body language used during each rendition, you must assess the credibility and believability of all persons corroborating some aspect of the complainant's or accused's contention, or providing a glimpse into the nature of their relationship.

In addition to presentation factors, consider the issue of witness motivation and the relationship between each witness and the individual whose word is being corroborated. Make sure you understand what each witness might stand to gain from the situation, as well as what genuine feelings ("This just isn't right," "I'm glad to be able to tell someone about this," "It's time someone did something about this," "People shouldn't be saying things that aren't true") are at work here.

Sheer numbers, of course, play a part in your final determination: If a clear majority supports one or the other party's position, this must be considered. But it is not a deciding factor. More important than numbers is the believability and honesty of the individuals you ultimately decide to rely on for your view of what actually occurred.

Preparing Signed Statements

Ask each individual you interview to help you draft a statement detailing your interview. Make sure each person reads the statement, and agrees that it is a fair and accurate representation of your discussion. Ask each corroborating witness to sign a statement once they've been typed up and read over. Place the original of each statement in the case file, with copies to each corroborating witness and to the investigator.

If a witness is reluctant to help you draft a statement, offer the time and private space needed to draft a statement by him or herself. Once drafted, review the language to make sure it reflects your conversation, have it typed and re-read, and ask the witness to sign it. Distribute the document as before, with the original to the case file and copies to the accused and the investigator.

If a witness refuses to consider a signed statement, draft one yourself, note the refusal to sign, and indicate that the statement represents your best understanding of the witness's position, based on your conversation.

9

Taking Corrective Action

Once all the parties have been interviewed, all relevant others have been met with, and all pertinent documents have been examined, the organization, relying on the completeness and soundness of the review conducted by its designated investigator, must decide what action it needs to take to both end any illegal or inappropriate conduct and restore harmony to the workplace. There is no easy set of instructions to follow in making the necessary judgments and assessments of both people and events; there is only the necessity to do so, and the advantage of as much information as a thorough investigation can yield, coupled with the judgment skills of a trained professional familiar with the organization and the people working in it.

While deciding the outcome in sexual harassment situations is not a scientific undertaking, the tools available are enough, for the employer is not a court and its ultimate judgment does not have to withstand judicial tests of evidence "beyond a reasonable doubt," or even "by a preponderance of the evidence." All the judgment must be is what it will be: based on all the facts a well-conducted investigation can uncover, along with the necessary refinements of those facts, based on the believability of the individuals presenting them. As long as this process includes both of those components, and the outcome is well reasoned and appropriate to the facts and circumstances uncovered, the result will hold.

Determining Whether Sexual Harassment Occurred

Making the Necessary Credibility Judgments

As the first step in making this determination, the employer carefully reviews the signed statements, the interview notes, and what was learned from reviewing the documentary evidence. It is not enough, however, to look just at the factual aspects of the situation; it is critical to make the softer judgments of credibility and believability that so many sexual harassment allegations turn on. Regardless of how uncomfortable it may be to sit in judgment on others, employers ignore this aspect of the decision at their peril.

Kestenbaum v. Pennzoil,[1] a 1988 New Mexico Supreme Court decision, illustrates what may happen if credibility issues are not fully addressed. Kestenbaum was in charge of operations at a secluded ranch owned by Pennzoil, and was accused of sexually harassing a young woman employee. An investigation was conducted involving interviews of past and present female employees. The accused was given two opportunities to present his version of the facts as well as respond to those of the complainant and to produce corroborating witnesses on his behalf. When the investigation was concluded, Kestenbaum was terminated for sexual harassment. Once discharged, Kestenbaum sued, alleging wrongful discharge.

The jury, after considering in detail the steps in the investigative process, decided that "Pennzoil did not act upon reasonable grounds" in terminating Kestenbaum on the basis of that investigation. While the steps were entirely proper, the investigation lacked one critical element: It made no attempt to evaluate the credibility of the individuals interviewed, or to separate firsthand knowledge from other, less valid forms of information such as hearsay, gossip, or rumor. As would most senior management officials, the decision makers in this case relied on oral briefings from the investigator as well as a written report; they did not conduct any independent verifications or, more important, review the investigation itself to make sure it was not flawed before relying on it. In this case, that failure cost Pennzoil some $500,000 in compensatory damages awarded to Kestenbaum for his wrongful discharge.

When It's "He Said, She Said"

Once the employer has reviewed the information and made the judgments required, it should compare the versions of various individuals, including the parties involved and any corroborating witnesses. If there are no corroborating witnesses, and there is only a blanket denial of guilt on the part of the accused, consider initiating another round of discussions—one that probes a little more deeply and presses a little more fully, depending on your reading of the personalities involved—to see if there might be more to the situation than appears at first glance. Consider discussing the issue of personal liability with the accused, to make sure he understands the possible consequences of sexual harassment actions. In this situation, it is reasonable to rely more extensively on documentary evidence.

Comparing With the EEOC Definition

When you've gone as far as you reasonably can, apply the Equal Employment Opportunity Commission's definition of sexual harassment to the facts and circumstances in your situation. Make sure you consider:

- Whether the conduct meets the "of a sexual nature" test or, if not overtly sexual in nature, it was prompted by the gender of the complainant—the "but for" alternative that satisfies this aspect of the test
- Whether the conduct was unwelcome to the complainant, even if there was voluntary participation on her part
- If a supervisor is the alleged harasser, whether there were tangible job benefits lost by the complainant as a result of the likely activity or whether, in their absence, the case turns on the notice provisions of a hostile-environment situation
- If a coworker is the alleged harasser, whether management knew or should have reasonably known of the

situation and, if so, what steps were taken to end the behavior

Looking at the Totality of the Circumstances

After establishing that conduct was both sexual in nature and unwelcome, the Equal Employment Opportunity Commission would, if it were reviewing a sexual harasssment situation, apply a totality-of-the-circumstances test to see whether the conduct involved rose to a level of legal sexual harassment. It's a good idea to use the same standard when reviewing your situation. Consider the most likely facts of your case against these elements:

- Whether and to what extent the complainant's terms and conditions of employment were affected.
- Whether the conduct was repeated or isolated.
- Whether the conduct was intended to be or was perceived to be serious or in a joking context.
- Whether the conduct is contrary to community standards and if so, to what degree. For this purpose, use the reasonable-person or reasonable-woman test if the latter has been adopted by your jurisdiction.

Based on the signed statements, the interview notes, the impressions of the investigator, and what was learned from the documentary evidence, and applying these factors, the employer should now be able to determine whether the actions in a particular case rise to a level of legal sexual harassment.

Involving Legal Counsel

If you have not already done so, now is the time to thoroughly brief the company's counsel on the allegation, the investigative steps taken, and the conclusions reached. Counsel should be shown all of the documents generated, including the interview notes, the signed statements, and any corporate records or other documents pertinent to the situation.

Thoroughly discuss the situation and alternative outcomes until both of you are comfortable with the proposed result and have planned how to handle any sensitive matters, particularly if termination is a possibility.

Meeting With Senior Management

As a prerequisite to taking action, arrange a meeting with the appropriate individuals from senior management, making sure that the group is as small as possible and that the manager responsible for the complainant and the accused is in attendance. Legal counsel may also wish to attend.

Orally brief senior management on the specific steps of the investigative process. Include a summary of each interview, along with your assessments of credibility and believability for each individual, and the reasons for them. Based on these factors, present your recommendations and ask senior management for a response. Be prepared for questions about the risks involved in each possible outcome, as well as the effect each might have on the work environment.

Once the group agrees on the actions to be taken, meet with the manager whose group is directly affected and agree on who will be responsible for implementing which aspects of the postinvestigation decisions, and when each will be addressed.

Postinvestigation Options

Employers have a wide range of options open to them after a sexual harassment investigation is completed. These generally can be grouped into two major categories: (1) those involving the imposition of some form of discipline and (2) those that do not.

Nondisciplinary Options

Among the options for employer action that do not have disciplinary consequences are:

- Counseling to help individuals cope more effectively with their work situations
- Mediation to help the parties resolve minor matters together
- Review of the Equal Employment Opportunity Commission guidelines on sexual harassment and/or the company's policy statement
- Redistribution of the company's policy statement to all employees
- Reeducation seminars for supervisors and managers (or all employees) about sexual harassment in the workplace

Disciplinary Options

The level of discipline appropriate in a given situation is affected by a number of factors. In addition to the facts and circumstances of the situation, consideration must be given to the severity of the conduct, how frequently it occurred, how pervasive it was, and whether there were prior complaints or incidents that might indicate a pattern or practice of sexual harassment. Possible disciplinary actions to be taken include:

- Suspension of the accused
- Transfer of the accused to a nonsupervisory position
- Written warning of termination if another incident or another instance of inappropriate conduct takes place, regardless of whether it rises to a level of legal sexual harassment
- Dismissal

Implementing the Postinvestigation Decision

Counseling and Mediation

Counseling may be the most appropriate outcome when the complainant:

- Makes allegations that clearly would not pass a reasonable-person test. An example of this kind of complaint is characterizing as sexual harassment the actions of a supervisor who bends over to see the complainant's computer screen, resting his arm on the back of her chair, or, satisfied with the results of his monitoring, gives her a pat on the shoulder before moving on to the next employee.

▪ Seems to be supersensitive, with an unreasonable definition of routine workplace actions as being sexual in nature.

▪ Misinterprets ordinary business behavior because of a difference in culture. An example of this is supervisory eye contact during work discussions, perceived as conduct that is sexual in nature.

▪ Misunderstands supervisory actions, or is dealing with only partial information, resulting in miscommunication. An example of this is a working dinner invitation construed as a date when, in fact, it is a working meeting or a group social event.

▪ Has indicated by past participation, past use of sexually oriented language, or past sexually oriented actions that sexual conduct at work is not unwelcome, has not indicated her change in feeling to those whose conduct she now finds offensive, and has experienced no increase in or escalation of that behavior in the workplace.

To resolve these situations, work with the complainant to correct misunderstandings and miscommunications, and to bring cultural or value differences out into the open. Make sure the complainant understands that whether or not conduct is illegal depends on a number of specific factors, including a reasonable, objective test. Conduct that is simply inappropriate is similarly governed by what most people consider natural and acceptable in a business setting. If you have not already done so, it may help to go over the Equal Employment Opportunity Commission's definition of sexual harassment, as well as the organization's policy statement prohibiting sexual harassment in the workplace. Remember that to be appropriate and defensible, outcomes do not have to necessarily provide the exact relief the complainant desired. What they must do is

be reasonable and effective in dealing with the situation alleged.

Similarly, counseling may be appropriate for the individual
accused of sexual misconduct when:

- He may be unaware of the effect of behavior he considers
to be perfectly reasonable and routine. An example of this type
of situation is the manager who touches all his employees,
male and female, in minor ways, such as an arm around the
shoulder, a pat on the back, or holding the employee's hand in
both of his. Usually, these are simply outgoing, good-natured
people who treat everyone with the same degree of warmth,
and who frequently inspire great personal loyalty and respect
among their subordinates. Yet some individuals find this conduct objectionable; to be safe, these managers need to understand that in today's climate their past behavior may put the
employer at risk. Counseling can help the person understand
this fact, and learn to better observe the signs that indicate
someone does not find the behavior comfortable.

- The accused has been in a past relationship with the
complainant, and is not aware that she no longer welcomes his
conduct, at work or outside of work. Counseling may help him
understand the seriousness of the situation, and the fact that
he may risk both disciplinary consequences as well as personal
liability should the unwelcome behavior continue.

- The accused is unaware of how the complainant views
even ordinary behavior, or behavior that may have different
connotations in the complainant's primary culture. Here, counseling can help the accused become more aware of the situation
and be more careful in dealing with the specific individual.

In any of these situations, but perhaps particularly when
the parties have a history together, if in your judgment bringing the two individuals together to discuss the situation might
resolve it, arrange for such a meeting when it is most likely to
be successful, usually after one or more individual meetings
with each party. In this situation, you function as the mediator,
setting the ground rules, allowing each person to present both

facts and feelings to the other, and moving the two toward a mutually agreeable resolution. Make sure that both individuals understand that if they are unable to reach an appropriate accord, the organization will take what it considers to be appropriate action instead.

Responding to Less Serious Situations

The vast middle ground of sexual harassment situations is somewhere between cases that require little more than one or two counseling sessions and those egregious circumstances where serious behavior must be met with serious corporate sanctions. Examples of less serious situations include:

- Circumstances in which there is no misunderstanding, miscommunicating, or supersensitivity, but there is a misreading of the complainant and her receptivity to kinds of behavior, such as unintentional jokes or teasing that are not degrading or derogatory to the complainant, in which the complainant is not singled out for special treatment, or in which there is minor or no touching involved
- Isolated or infrequent instances of teasing, joking, visual displays, sexually oriented language, or minor nonintimate touching
- Circumstances involving no tangible job-benefit losses or only minor interference with the employee's ability to work in the environment
- Inconclusive situations involving substantially equal support from both facts and assessments of credibility

In these situations it may be appropriate, depending on the facts and circumstances, to resolve the situation with nondisciplinary measures, less serious disciplinary actions, or a combination of the two.

At a minimum, consider reviewing the Equal Employment Opportunity Commission's definition of sexual harassment and the company's own policy statement with the accused individual. Make sure there is agreement on the level of behavior appropriate in a business setting and obtain a pledge to adhere to that behavior in the future. Remind the accused of the organization's pledge of nonretaliation toward the complainant and elicit agreement that it will be followed.

Future monitoring of the situation in these less serious circumstances accomplishes two things. First, the prospect of monitoring should give the complainant some reassurance that her allegations have been taken seriously and that the complained-of behavior will cease. Second, the monitoring will remind the accused that he has been placed on notice that the organization will not tolerate sexual harassment of its employees, and that someone with knowledge of this situation will be watching.

If the facts and circumstances warrant, consider placing a memo in the accused's personnel file that states simply that a sexual harassment allegation was raised on a given date, against this individual, and that after a complete investigation, results were inconclusive. In the event a similar situation develops later, this notice may help the employer implement a higher level of discipline than might have been possible without the prior documentation.

In resolving these situations, it is usually most useful to focus on the future rather than on the past. After all, the employer's obligation is to end the illegal or inappropriate behavior and to provide a harassment-free workplace for its employees. If the employer attempts to adjudicate the past, without benefit of an investigation that substantiates a credible, corroborated, and serious allegation, it is likely to decrease the possibility of a reasoned, mutual resolution and increase the likelihood of litigation from both parties.

One of the ways employers can help themselves in these gray situations is to offer to implement some changes in the complainant's work situation that might increase her comfort level as well as make a recurrence of the problem less likely. These changes might include making permanent any interim measures put into place during the investigation or developing a new approach now that the investigation is over. Usually, this form of relief involves moving of one or the other party to another location or another job function.

If transferring the coworker or supervisor against whom the complaint was lodged is possible, this may well be the better practice, particularly if there is questionable activity that may not rise to the level of sexual harassment. The job offered should involve approximately the same level of responsibility and possibilities for advancement, and the compensation level should be maintained.

If moving the alleged harasser is not feasible, offer the complainant the possibility of a transfer, making sure she understands that she is under no coercion or compulsion to accept. The new job should provide the same level of responsibility, the same degree of opportunity for advancement, at the same compensation. Whether or not the complainant accepts, the company will have demonstrated its good faith and its willingness to provide the complainant with an alternative work situation. Should she later resign and allege that her working environment was rendered intolerable because of harassment, leaving her no choice but to leave (a claim of constructive discharge), the company may be able to defeat that claim using its transfer offer as evidence.

Whether the complainant accepts the offer to transfer or elects to remain in her current job situation, the employer should take one additional step in these gray situations: ongoing monitoring and follow-up activity to ensure there is no retaliation and no harassment activity in the future. Since the employer is now on notice as to the potential problem, failure to take preventive action may be costly.

Responding to More Serious Situations

When the facts and circumstances lead to the conclusion that there has been a serious breach of the obligation to provide a workplace free of sexual harassment, the employer's response needs to more serious. Examples of these situations include:

- A repetitive pattern of behavior aimed specifically at the complainant
- When the accused understood or, based on the circum-

stances, should have understood that his conduct was unwelcome, but he persisted in his attentions
- When there was a tangible job-benefit loss linked to some sexually oriented activity
- Intimate physical contact that was unwelcome
- When sexuality, even if consensual, permeated the workplace and affected the performance of the complainant, to whom it was unwelcome

In these serious situations, the employer is expected to mete out serious discipline, up to and including dismissal, if warranted. Depending on the facts and any mitigating circumstances, lesser discipline than termination may be selected. At minimum, if a supervisor is involved he should be removed from his position and transferred to one in which he will have no further responsibility for managing others. In addition, a period of suspension without pay should be imposed or there should be an official reprimand that clearly states that dismissal will occur if another situation of demonstrated sexually inappropriate behavior occurs later.

For many of these situations, termination is the preferred remedy when the investigation has provided credible corroboration for a serious allegation or when there appears to be a pattern with respect to the accused, even if the level of individual offenses may be somewhat less serious.

While termination—the "corporal punishment" of the workplace—is a serious matter, the employer runs far less risk in terminating when appropriate than in either retaining the employee or permitting him to resign. For instance, if the employer retains the employee and the behavior recurs, either with this or another complainant, the employer may face a civil suit claiming negligent retention. That is, since the employer knew of the prior behavior, it also should have foreseen that there would be a risk of future behavior, and should have taken appropriate actions to prevent it.

Permitting an employee to resign rather than face termination may be an equally poor decision. While employers may be swayed by misplaced compassion, or be reluctant to handle what they believe will be an angry confrontation, administrative agency investigators and juries invariably conclude that the only reason the employer failed to terminate was because it did not feel it had enough evidence to do so. This weakens the employer's position significantly, should the terminated employee later file a charge or begin a civil lawsuit.

When termination is the answer, it should be carried out by the individual's direct supervisor, in a meeting attended by the designated investigator. Spend as much time as is needed with the terminating manager to make sure he understands the ramifications of the situation, and stress that he use appropriate language in informing the individual of his separation.

The termination meeting should be brief, devoted to conveying the clear, unambiguous message that, based on the facts and circumstances uncovered in the course of the investigation, the company believes that his conduct has been inappropriate in a business setting (if a supervisory employee is involved, the terminating manager may also want to state that his conduct was not an authorized exercise of the power the corporation vested in him to supervise a group of employees on its behalf) and that a corporate decision has been reached to terminate his employment with the company, effective on the named date.

Resist any attempts to discuss the matter in any greater detail and arrange for when, and under what circumstances, the employee will leave the premises. As in any other termination situation, avoid belittling the employee, stripping him of his dignity or labeling his conduct in a prejudicial way.

If possible, have someone available immediately, preferably a trained outside facilitator, to deal with the individual's anger and feelings of betrayal, and to reinforce the fact of the termination. Although this last step is optional, it is sound business practice that significantly decreases the chances of later litigation by helping the individual accept and deal with his termination.

Make sure the terminated employee either has in his hand his final paycheck and written information on his employee benefits, or that he's told specifically when these will be mailed. Rather than return the terminated employee to his workspace, schedule the session for the afternoon. Let him and his counselor use a neutral conference room for the balance of the day, and let him know when his personal belongings will be sent to him. Before he leaves, make sure all keys, corporate identification cards, company property, and/or computer passwords are obtained or scheduled to be changed.

As long as the employer has conducted a proper investigation, and has taken what it sincerely believes to be appropriate action based on its findings, it will generally be able to defend its position in any subsequent action brought by the employee terminated because of sexual harassment. In *Jackson v. St. Joseph State Hospital*,[2] for example, the postinvestigation discipline imposed on the male supervisor was a warning to avoid touching female subordinates, discussing their personal lives with them, or disciplining them without a third party present. The supervisor's reverse sex-discrimination complaint resulted in a finding for the employer. Similarly, in *Carosella v. U.S. Postal Service*,[3] the male supervisor was removed from his position because the employer believed he had created a hostile work environment. His denial-of-due-process argument was rejected by the court.

A last argument for termination is, of course, the cathartic effect it may have on the remaining employees as well as the clear message it sends to all observers. Termination says that the company takes sexual harassment seriously and will provide disciplinary sanctions it considers appropriate, including termination of employment.

Responding to Situations Involving Outsiders

When sexual harassment allegations involve outsiders—suppliers or vendors, visitors or guests, even customers—both investigation and outcome options are more limited. It is not likely that an interview with the accused will be possible, nor is the employer necessarily in a position to demand, or even request, that the individual listen to the allegations, let alone cooperate to resolve the situation. To compound the problem, there often are delicate business relationships involved, particularly when customers are the focus of the complaint.

A realistic course of action to minimize the employer's risk and to effect some real change in future encounters between the alleged harasser and the complaining employee might be to acquaint a senior manager with the allegations and ask him to deal directly with his counterparts in the other company, or with the individual if no other organization is involved.

When the employer is the customer, as with vendors and suppliers, a phone call to the account representative is often successful in transferring the offending employee from this account, as well as putting the service firm on notice that future infractions by the same or other personnel will result in withdrawal of the employer's business.

When the customer is the harasser, the situation is much more difficult, yet the subject must be broached. This should be done by a senior official, in a tactful and discreet way that offends the customer least. Hypothetical or jocular approaches have worked successfully, getting the point across while preserving the business relationship. As long as the employer takes steps to end such conduct in the future, including possibly meeting the customer out of the office, assigning a male employee to meet and greet, or otherwise minimizing future contact between the complaining employee and the customer, and as long as the employer explains the situation to the complainant, the employer's obligations have probably been met.

Closing the Communication Loop

Responding to Employee Questions

In transfer or termination situations, care must be taken in responding to questions from other employees in the workgroup. Terminating managers should be cautioned that overcommunicating the investigation results to those who really have no business need to know them is a sure way for the employer to lose its qualified privilege and expose itself to actions for damage to the individual's reputation and good name. This is just as true when those involved are fellow employees concerned about the welfare of the transferred or terminated individual.

To balance this concern with the employer's needs, and to minimize discussion of the matter among employees in the work unit, the terminating manager should respond to specific one-on-one questions with a simple, factual statement such as "X is now working in the _____ department," or "X is no longer working here." Managers should avoid any kind of group meeting, even with only two or three people, and should bypass any characterization, opinion, or even factual information as to the reason for corporate action.

Updating the Complainant

A case can (and perhaps should) be made that informing the complainant of the actions taken against the accused is not publication to an individual who does not need to know the facts. The chances for an effective resolution of the situation are increased when the complainant is told, at least in general terms, of what actions have been taken with respect to the accused, as well as what is now expected of her.

Reversing Any Tainted Actions

If it seems likely that certain supervisory actions were tainted by sexual harassment, give serious consideration to reversing those actions, whether they involve salary increases, promotions, job assignments, or terminations. Corporate failure to correct such situations can be costly. In *Yates v. Avco Corp.*,[4] the company, after investigating the sexual harassment allegations brought by two female employees, concluded that its supervisor had in fact sexually harassed these employees. Yet it resisted changing absence records made part of the personnel file, even though it was well aware that one of the employees had been absent as a result of the harassment activity.

Early in the investigative phase of the case, Avco had placed its supervisor on administrative leave pending the investigation's conclusion. When one of the complainants requested such a leave for herself, and while the supervisor was still on site, she was first told it could be arranged, but then the request was denied; instead, the company's personnel manager told her to call in sick and to obtain a doctor's note for each such "illness." Since her doctor refused to fabricate the notes, her personnel file contained a signficant number of absences for this period. The personnel information was not changed, even after the supervisor was demoted and transferred to another location, until ordered amended by the court.

As part of the general follow-up to an investigation, identify any such actions and provide an effective remedy to remove any taint promptly.

Documenting the Files

The case file should be closed with a copy of the personnel action taken: a termination notice, a notice of transfer, a putting-the-accused-on-notice memo. Any reversals of corporate actions should also be included, with the relevant forms. The investigator's notes of disciplinary or termination meetings, and notes of meetings with senior management and/or legal counsel should also be included. The file should be stored where access is restricted to those directly involved with sensitive employee issues.

The personnel files of those involved in sexual harassment situations should be documented with the "inconclusive" result memo described earlier, or with personnel forms the employer has completed to take disciplinary action, such as the transfer form or termination form. A separate memo describing the action taken is both unnecessary and unwise; let the corporate action speak for itself.

Responding to Reference Checks

The Neutral-Reference Policy

Traditionally, employers have been told that the best defense for any litigation resulting from an inquiry into a current or former employee by a prospective employer or credit grantor is to do and say essentially nothing. Most employers take that advice to heart and restrict their responses to the dates an employee worked for the company and the employee's last job title. This is called a "neutral" reference policy, because the employer provides only basic information and refrains from expressing an opinion or elaborating on such normal areas of inquiry as reason for leaving, performance in the job, and whether or not the company would rehire the individual. While there can be no safeguard against an uneducated manager with the gift of gab, this policy was, up until recently, quite effective in reducing an employer's exposure to defamation claims.

Compelled Self-Publication

Recently, a Minnesota court created a new defamation doctrine called compelled self-publication. This has, and will continue to have, far-reaching effects on what can and should be reported to inquiring third parties. In the case of first impression, *Lewis, et al. v. Equitable Life Assurance Society of the United States,*[5] a small group of claims approvers refused to alter their expense reports for a lengthy stay in another state, where, at the employer's request, they had helped reduce claim backlog. Receiving no information about proper expense report items or amounts before they left, on their return to Minnesota the group proceeded to list recreational and other noncovered or excessive items for reimbursement, refusing to alter their forms to conform with corporate practice or follow their manager's suggestion to just list expenses under item names or categories that were reimbursable. The individuals were ultimately terminated for gross misconduct.

The employer, adhering to its neutral reference policy, said nothing concerning the former employees. However, the employees, when searching for other employment, were faced with the choice of either accurately answering application questions about their termination or lying to their prospective employers, a choice forced on them, in the court's view, by the corporation's very silence. That silence compelled the individuals to publish the negative information about themselves, since the alternative—lying on application forms and in interviews for employment—cannot be encouraged as a matter of public policy. Here, following a neutral-reference policy resulted in a judgment against the employer of some $300,000 in compensatory and over $3 million in punitive damages, largely because the underlying termination was based on questionable circumstances handled in a poor manner.

Following Minnesota's lead, the doctrine of compelled self-publication has been recognized by Michigan, California, and New York, making it a force to warrant serious consideration. The message to employers in general—and those in these states in particular—is that neutral-reference policies need to be reexamined since they may, in fact, increase potential liability under this doctrine. In essence, the failure of a company to provide truthful, detailed termination reasons, particularly in ambiguous or unflattering situations, forces the employee to disclose the reason given for dismissal, which may itself be unsupportable or at variance with the reason given to the employee at the time of termination.

For example, if an employer is unwise enough to terminate someone for "being a sexual harasser" without the concrete proof required to use such a defamatory label, in a compelled self-publication state the neutral-reference policy may add to the company's risk of a high dollar judgment.

Negligent Referral

Another, related issue signaling the imminent demise of the neutral-reference policy is a new tort, just beginning to be talked about, called negligent referral. As the name implies, the prospective employer, attempting to check the references of a job applicant and avoid negligent hiring risks, is effectively prevented from doing so by the refusal of the referencing employer to provide anything other than the "name, rank, and serial number" permitted by a neutral-reference policy. If the hired employee engages in conduct that causes harm in the new workplace, the second employer will argue that it would never have hired the individual had it been apprised of that same behavior by the first employer. It is not beyond the realm of possibility that the first employer can be held liable for full damages in such situations if it fails to disclose the behavior at issue, when asked.

A Suggested Alternative

For reasons of both compelled self-publication and negligent referral, employers need to review their existing reference policies and consider replacing their neutral-reference position with a policy that relies on the employer's qualified privilege to tell the truth to those with a reasonable need to hear it. The preferable procedure is:

1. Channel all requests for reference information to a central source, making sure there is a mechanism for alerting responders to sensitive situations.
2. Require that all requests for reference information be made in writing, whether responding in kind or over the phone. That way, the employer retains a record of the transaction, and knows with whom it is dealing. Particularly in sensitive situations, reference requests should never be accepted over the phone.
3. Make sure that responders understand the difference between a fact and an opinion, between characterization or innuendo. This is particularly critical in sexual harassment situations, when the language used must be accurate and objective, not sensationalized or careless. The statement "Mr. Doe was terminated for sexual harassment" or "Mr. Doe is a sexual harasser" is far different from "As a result of a sexual harassment investigation, the company decided to terminate Mr. Doe's employment, even though the results of the investigation were inconclusive."
4. Make sure all supervisors and managers know where to refer reference inquiries within the organization and recognize the difference between fact and opinion, since employment checks will invariably find their way through the company maze to the employee's last direct supervisor.

5. Make sure that every employee has signed a release permitting the corporation to respond fully to legitimate reference inquiries. The ideal time to obtain this permission is on the application form itself, rather than at the time of termination.

NOTES

1. 766 P.2d 280.
2. No. 86–2595 (8th Cir. March 1, 1988).
3. 816 F.2d 638, 43 FEP Cases 845 (Fed. Cir. 1987).
4. No. 86–5288 (6th Cir. May 21, 1987).
5. 1 IER Cases 1269 (Minn. Sup. Ct. 1986).

10

Policy as Prevention

A well-drafted, carefully thought-out policy statement on sexual harassment can be valuable to an organization in at least three major ways: (1) as an employee relations tool, (2) as basic education for both managers and employees on the subject of sexual harassment, and (3) as a way of minimizing legal liability to the organization in hostile-environment sexual harassment cases.

As an employee relations tool, the policy statement clearly indicates the employer's concern for the well-being of its employees at work, and its commitment to providing a work environment free of harassment or of inappropriate behavior and language that may make employees uncomfortable. A well-administered procedure for dealing with sexual harassment situations should also increase employee awareness and reliance on internal dispute-resolution processes when these are viewed as credible, even-handed mechanisms. Policy statements can, therefore, increase the likelihood of the internal resolution of problems before government agencies, attorneys, and courts become involved. Such internal resolution certainly results in greater organizational control over the situation as well as considerable savings in legal and administrative costs.

As a method of providing fundamental education on the subject of sexual harassment for both managers and employees, a policy statement can provide clear guidelines for workplace behavior by defining what sexual harassment is (and, just as important, what it is not). By making everyone aware of the rules, policy statements also significantly reduce the chances of harassment occurring, especially inadvertently.

But well-drafted, well-communicated policies may be most important as tools for limiting employer legal liability, or, under the right set of facts, cutting liability off entirely. Not only is such a policy statement evidence of an organization's good-faith effort to provide a work environment free of harassment but, coupled with a proper investigation that successfully ends illegal or inappropriate conduct, it provides a major offensive weapon in employer efforts to demonstrate that all reasonable steps were taken and that they were effective.

Elements of an Effective Policy Statement

It Is a Separate, Written Document

Many organizations prefer to include sexual harassment issues as part of a general policy statement on Equal Employment Opportunity matters, or as part of a policy statement on all forms of harassment in the workplace. One of the reasons usually given is the unwillingness to call what is considered "undue" attention to the sensitive area of sexual harassment by breaking it out into a separate topic.

Inclusive treatment, however, runs the risk of burying a message employers need to send, and employees want to hear, so that both the employee relations and the legal advantages of the policy are not fully achieved. Not only is separate attention desirable in this situation, it is justified by the unique aspects of sexual harassment in contrast to other Title VII claims. A separate policy also indicates the seriousness that management accords the subject, and reinforces the message that this conduct will not be tolerated.

Since the policy is a written document—part of a policy manual issued to supervisors and managers as well as included in an employee handbook or guide—it is subject to the same risks any other written material carries in today's legal climate. Employers must be prepared to implement their policies uniformly and consistently to avoid breach-of-contract claims for failure to act or for unequal treatment of offenders. And, of course, a policy statement will not insulate an employer that ignores sexual harassment charges or obvious situations, or that fails to follow its own policies or procedures.

It Contains a Clear Definition

While it may be tempting simply to replicate the three-part definition of sexual harassment contained in the Equal Employment Opportunity Commission guidelines, spend some time and effort simplifying that language to create a statement that is clear and written in plain English rather than in legalese. The goal is simple: Make sure that all employees will understand what the law defines as sexual harassment, as well as what incidents the organization would like brought to its attention. For example, the following rewritten definition is easier to understand (and more likely to be read and remembered) than the formal language of the commission's guidelines:

At _____ Company, we believe that employees should be able to work in an environment that is free of all forms of harassment, particularly those involving:

- Unwelcome sexual advances in return for money, promotions, or other workplace opportunities
- Workplace decisions affecting your employment when you believe these were made because of your reactions to those kinds of advances
- The nature of your work environment, if you believe the atmosphere you work in has been made hostile, intimidating, or offensive to you by the actions of others

If any of these are a concern, the company has a need to know about the circumstances that are affecting your performance or making you uncomfortable at work.[1]

Another way of structuring a policy statement definition so that it is understandable to everyone is to track the commission's guidelines but include examples of prohibited conduct. If examples are used, include disclaimer language that clearly states the conduct portrayed in the examples is not all-inclusive but only illustrative. While examples do clarify the types of behavior prohibited, they may also lead employees to think that only those behaviors are considered sexual harassment, rather than any number of behaviors depending on the parties and the circumstances.

Although it fails to mention harassment from nonemployees, AT&T's sexual harassment policy is interesting for its attempt to track the EEOC definition with relevant examples added:

> AT&T's sexual harassment policy prohibits sexual harassment in the workplace, whether committed by supervisory or non-supervisory personnel. Specifically, no supervisor shall threaten to insinuate, either explicitly or implicitly, that an employee's submission to or rejection of sexual advances will in any way influence any personnel decision regarding that employee's employment, wages, advancement, assigned duties, shifts, or any other condition of employment or career development.
>
> Other sexually harassing conduct in the workplace that may create an offensive work environment, whether it be in the form of physical or verbal harassment, and regardless of whether committed by supervisory or non-supervisory personnel, is also prohibited. This includes, but is not limited to, repeated offensive or unwelcome sexual flirtations, advances, propositions, continual or repeated verbal abuse of a sexual nature, graphic verbal commentaries about an individual's body; sexually degrading words used to describe an individual; and the display in the workplace of sexually suggestive objects or pictures.[2]

Whatever techniques are used to promote clarity of language and better understanding, the content of the policy definition should closely track the guidelines of the Equal

Employment Opportunity Commission. These have the advantage of consistency with federal court decisions and generally receive considerable deference from the courts, the agencies, and the plaintiff bar.

It Provides an Effective Resolution Procedure

Employers with viable, credible complaint-resolution procedures for other employee-relations issues—such as equal opportunity concerns, appeals of performance reviews, or employee questions or complaints—should resolve sexual harassment matters in the same way as much as possible. This approach has the added legal advantage of providing equal treatment for all types of employee complaints, including sexual harassment.

If an employer's internal complaint-resolution mechanisms are nonexistent, ignored, or disfunctional, the company needs to consider providing an alternative, effective procedure for sexual harassment situations that is different from the mainstream complaint procedure. The small risk of opening the organization to claims of disparate treatment may well be offset by the benefits of prompt notification and the opportunity to resolve these disputes internally before others become involved. Not only could such a revised procedural mechanism effectively limit the employer's liability in sexual harassment cases, but it might also serve as a model to resuscitate the employer's mainstream internal dispute-resolution programs so that all employee complaints can be credibly and effectively resolved. Alternative treatments can be justified where, as in sexual harassment cases, all the parties involved—the accuser, the accused, the witnesses, the investigator, management personnel and the organization itself—have rights and obligations that may well conflict. The employer should take any steps it can to make it easy and nonthreatening for employees to bring sexual harassment concerns to the attention of the organization.

It Directs Employees to a Neutral Party

To be credible and effective, as well as to provide maximum legal protection to the employer, a company's sexual harassment policy should never direct employees with a claim, a concern, or even a question to their immediate supervisor. Since case law and common sense both tell us that the immediate supervisor is the person most likely to be the accused, or to have failed to notice or to have actively ignored evidence of a hostile-environment situation, policy statements that send employees to their supervisors for counseling or complaint resolution are viewed unfavorably by most courts as well as by the Equal Employment Opportunity Commission. As a practical matter, the lack of a credible alternative also considerably lessens the employer's chances of receiving the information it needs to take appropriate action, and therefore lessens the chances of resolving the situation internally before administrative or civil charges are filed.

Policy statements should direct inquiries and complaints on sexual harassment or other sensitive workplace issues to a designated management ombudsman or human resources professional trained to deal with these issues and with the organizational clout to resolve them.

It Emphasizes Action

An effective policy statement on sexual harassment should clearly articulate the organization's goal in responding to any and all reports of incidents. That goal is simply to end any illegal conduct and to see that it does not recur. How the organization accomplishes that objective is through prompt and thorough investigation of every allegation, leading to action on any misconduct the investigation uncovers. Again, employers that want to maximize their legal protections need to be prepared to deliver on these assurances, not merely state them as policy.

It Talks About Consequences

Policy statements should include at least two areas of possible disciplinary consequences for employees. Not only is this a clear warning that helps employers in any defamation or wrongful termination case, but it also is a strong indication of how the organization feels about sexual harassment in the workplace. The policy should state that appropriate levels of discipline, up to and including dismissal, may result, depending on the findings of the investigation.

Disciplinary consequences should also be raised in terms of conduct not defined as sexual harassment but that weakens the company's ability to effectively defuse the situation as well as leaves it open to suits for defamation. That conduct, of course, involves spreading information about the sexual harassment claim, its participants, or its investigation and resolution—whether that information is accurate or not. Employees need to understand that allegations of sexual harassment are serious and have potentially far-reaching consequences, in terms of both employer discipline and broader legal concerns involving personal as well as corporate liability. While it is probably more effective to discuss the need for minimal communication to others as part of the investigative process, it should also be touched on in the policy statement.

It Does Not Guarantee Confidentiality

Since sexual harassment issues are so sensitive, and employees may hesitate before discussing them with comparative strangers, many employers try to encourage employees to come forward with a promise of confidentiality in their policy statements. Because of the legal duties involved, and the frequent conflicts of rights, obligations, and even facts, sexual harassment allegations will never be held in strict confidence, and promises to do so only undermine the complaint-resolution system and give employees a reason to distrust management. Since the company has the duty to investigate every allegation—whether or not the complainant wants a review done and whether or not the complainant will cooperate in the investigation—obviously a number of other persons will have to be acquainted with the situation.

In lieu of a pledge of strict confidentiality, policy statements should say that concerns will be kept as confidential as possible, or that every effort will be made to limit both the number of people who need to know and the extent of any discussion. Coupled with strong language that unauthorized disclosure of facts or opinions is prohibited and has disciplinary consequences, this need-to-know limitation should reassure employees while protecting the organization's ability to conduct the investigation required.

It Pledges Nonretaliation

While policy statements need to avoid promising a level of confidentiality that cannot be honored, they should always include assurances that employees who bring sexual harassment to management's attention will be protected from retaliatory action. Title VII's prohibition against retaliation for the exercise of rights granted by the statute applies, as does the general judicial tendency to find basic unfairness in unfavorable consequences for a good-faith belief in accordance with an employer's own policy.

It has been repeatedly held that employers may not discipline or otherwise adversely affect the terms and conditions of employment of an employee who sincerely but mistakenly believes that sexual harassment has occurred and who brings that belief to the attention of the organization. Only when it is clear that the employee is motivated by spite or malice, and is using the complaint-resolution system for personal revenge, is the employer justified in imposing discipline, up to and including termination.

Consistency With Other Policies

Format and Style

Sexual harassment policies should be written in the same format and style as are other company policy statements, including matters of length and content.

Conflict-of-Interest Policies

These policies represent another opportunity for employers to emphasize to supervisors and managers the need for appropriate conduct at work. The company can do so by explaining that sexual affairs between managers and employees under their supervision is a conflict of interest. Such a statement reinforces the idea that poor managerial judgment in even consensual workplace affairs may affect the performance of others in the work group, who may perceive favoritism or the sharing of confidential information, or who may claim a hostile work environment. Consider requiring disclosure of such involvements annually, just as disclosures of business dealings and stock ownership are now common. They provide the employer with the knowledge to decide whether any action should be taken to safeguard the organization.

Employee Privacy Policies

Privacy for employees has recently become a much talked about legal issue, centering on health and performance matters but also including search and records retention policies. For most private employers, it is still true that employees leave their constitutional rights, including freedom of speech and freedom from searches, at the workplace door. They have only such rights as are granted to them specifically through legislative action, union and individual contracts, case law, and, of course, the employer's own policies and procedures, whether embodied in a policy manual or evidenced in past practice.

Employers should, therefore, review for consistency with their sexual harassment policy any other policy statements that might contain language on employee privacy or confidentiality. Examples include policies on AIDS, drug testing, medical and personnel records, telephone and computer monitoring of performance, and searches of desks and lockers, etc.

Antinepotism Policies

Employers interested in protecting themselves from personnel actions that could inadvertently result in Title VII violations will want to learn of consensual affairs between supervisors and subordinates and can use conflict-of-interest and/or sexual harassment policy statements to help do so. Review any existing policy on nepotism that forbids spouses and close relatives from working in a supervisory-subordinate relationship. Make sure that marital status is not dealt with more severely than situations involving unmarried employees in the same position who are living together or are involved in a "significant other" relationship.

Give consideration to liberalizing the language or the implementation of an antinepotism policy, as well as to granting exceptions to the policy if desirable. Agencies and courts will not look with favor on employers whose policies cause disparate impact on the basis of marital status while tolerating the same relationship between two unmarried but intimate employees.

As with so much in employee relations, it is critical how employers go about learning of matters many employees feel are none of the organization's business. How successful employers are probably depends on how well they explain their business need for that information, as well as how it will (and will not) be used, and what level of trust employees already have in their organization's desire to do the right thing. Approached carefully and candidly, and with an eye toward balancing the organization's need to know with the manager's desire to keep personal matters personal, these subjects can be discussed to the mutual benefit of all concerned.

Distributing the Policy Statement

The most carefully drafted, best-written policy on sexual harassment is useless if it is not communicated throughout the organization. Depending on the type of business and the way other information is disseminated to employees, organizations may want to consider taking the following steps:

• Include the sexual harassment policy in the employee handbook, not just in management's policy manual. For the policy to accomplish both its preventive and its protective objectives, it must be distributed to all employees—the population expected to generate the majority of claims, concerns, or inquiries. Since employee handbooks should be reviewed and revised on a regular basis, at least annually, it may be convenient to include a new policy on sexual harassment with other new statements. This achieves the company's objectives without singling out the topic.

- Use any appropriate occasion to reinforce the basic message, including new-employee orientation, handbook revision discussions, and appropriate training sessions. Rather than simply hand employees a written document, use these times to orally review the policy materials—again, as part of a number of topics covered in that way.

- Make sure supervisors and managers are aware of the policy, as well as of the organization's position on sexual harassment in general. Develop a way to run new supervisors and managers through training on this matter along with other need-to-know basics early on in their new positions.

- Ask senior management to mention the policy and the company's commitment to it in an appropriate and natural way at management meetings or off-site seminars.

- Always caution managers against discussing specific cases or situations, even for training or education purposes, unless care has been taken to minimize the risk of defamation from overbroad communications, even of facts or events.

Prevention at Its Best

Preventing sexual harassment from occurring is much less disruptive, much less expensive, and much less time-consuming than investigating and/or litigating these incidents. The single most effective tool in the prevention arsenal is a well-drafted, well-communicated policy statement that follows the guidelines in this chapter. Other ways an employer can help itself through prevention strategies are contained in the next chapter.

NOTES

1. "How to Write a Sexual Harassment Policy" (Red Bank, N.J.: Creative Solutions Press, 1990). Reprinted courtesy of Creative Solutions, Inc.
2. Stephanie Strom, "Harassment Cases Can Go Unnoticed," *New York Times*, October 20, 1991, p. 22.

11

Other Prevention Strategies

Employers who make the effort to prevent sexual harassment from occurring can benefit by avoiding a host of potential problems. Because of the high emotionalism usually involved, embarrassment or fear of coming forward, and the lack of witnesses, sexual harassment allegations are often harder to resolve satisfactorily than other employee claims. Even when changes are promptly made, followed by a speedy investigation, people's positions tend to harden and it becomes more difficult to mediate an agreement as time passes.

The sensitive nature of the claim also raises emotions in third-party advisors or influencers, such as spouses, friends, relatives, and coworkers. Their personal feelings often run as high as those of the parties involved, and their conduct may be less amenable to the checks of workplace relationships and first-person knowledge of the situation. In *Koster v. Chase Manhattan Bank,*[1] for instance, after a decision denying a claim of hostile-environment sexual harassment on the basis that the plaintiff's affair with her supervisor was welcomed, the plaintiff's father killed the judge and then committed suicide. Cases such as this, and their attendant unfavorable publicity for the employer, underscore the importance of effective prevention strategies.

Taking steps to prevent sexual harassment before it occurs benefits the organization in many practical ways as well. Dealing with a sexual harassment claim may disrupt the work environment, result in unnecessary tension and damaged work relationships, divert time and effort that could otherwise be used for business production, and cost money for legal fees. Prevention is easier, cleaner, and much less expensive.

Most courts agree with the broad interpretation of how far employers should go in their prevention efforts, contained in the Equal Employment Opportunity Commission's guidelines:

> Prevention is the best tool for the elimination of sexual harassment. An employer should take all steps necessary to prevent sexual harassment from occurring, such as affirmatively raising the subject, expressing strong disapproval, developing appropriate sanctions, informing employees of their right to raise the issue of harassment under Title VII and developing methods to sensitize all concerned.[2]

In the last chapter we looked at one of the most important prevention tools: a well-drafted, well-communicated policy statement on sexual harassment. Prudent employers can, however, do more both through education and training, and by implementation of strategies to encourage employee communication of sexual harassment concerns through appropriate corporate channels.

Training: An Important Prevention Strategy

For Managers and Supervisors

Anyone who supervises others, even if only a single employee, needs to have some basic education in a number of employee-relations areas, including sexual harassment. Ideally, all supervisors and managers should have a fundamental knowledge of equal opportunity and affirmative action issues, the provisions of Title VII and its impact on the workplace, as well as the revolution in employer-employee relationships caused by the judicial erosion of the employment-at-will doctrine in many state jurisdictions. Basic information on the theory and application of the organization's human resources policies will also help managers better understand the many factors that go into situational decision making as well as the fact that personnel decisions have consequences both for the individuals involved and also for the organization.

Training that supervisors and managers should receive in the area of sexual harassment should include:

- What sexual harassment is and what it is not, from both legal and practical points of view
- The difference between sexual harassment and inappropriate conduct, and why both need to be banned from the workplace
- The types of sexual harassment and the implications for employer and personal liability of each
- How internal investigations are triggered and what happens during such an investigation
- The need for minimizing any discussion of sexual harassment situations, both formally and informally
- The legal and organizational requirement for nonretaliation against those who raise sexual harassment concerns
- The corporate options for postinvestigation discipline and the factors that decision makers use in selecting that discipline
- External charge mechanisms (Equal Employment Opportunity Commission complaints and civil lawsuits) and how these generally proceed
- What every supervisor and manager is expected to do in his or her own area to prevent sexual harassment from occurring, whether in terms of personal behavior, co-worker relationships, or visitor conduct
- Who the designated organizational person to receive reports of possible sexual harassment is, and the need for early reporting

In addition, supervisors and managers need to have an interpersonal or behavior-awareness component in their training. Done either through group discussion, critiques of video vignettes, or gender-switching role playing, this softer kind of training is necessary to:

- Raise awareness of the more subtle forms of sexual harassment.

- Make supervisors and managers more sensitive to differences in perception between the sexes. Women tend to rate even routine language and behavior in the workplace as more sexually serious than do men. Women also tend to consider less severe forms of behavior as sexual in nature, or as a form of sexual harassment, while men may not.

- Have supervisors experience, to the extent possible, the feelings of both the accuser and the accused. This technique reveals the true nature of sexual harassment as power based rather than sexual behavior, which most frequently results in feelings of degradation and low self-esteem.

For Employees

As with supervisors and managers, all employees should receive some information on sexual harassment in the workplace. For employees as a whole, the emphasis should be on expectations for interpersonal behavior rather than on legal and management issues. Such training sessions should include:

- Clear examples or video vignettes of what sexual harassment is and what it is not
- Strong messages by credible, high-ranking corporate officials that sexual harassment will not be tolerated by the organization
- Encouragement to come forward and discuss sexual harassment concerns if and when they arise, with clear directions as to where to take these issues
- Review of the organization's policy statement on sexual harassment, with emphasis on the investigative process and possible disciplinary outcomes

For Investigators

The soundness of a sexual harassment investigaton and the comfort the organization will feel with its results largely depend on the quality of the fact-finding process itself. Investigations are frequently emotion-laden, highly charged events with high stakes for those involved. To do an effective job, the staff members likely to conduct a sexual harassment investigation should be thoroughly trained in:

- The legal definition of sexual harassment as interpreted by the Equal Employment Opportunity Commission and the various courts
- The employer's legal obligations, and the best ways of discharging them
- Questioning techniques designed to elicit explanations of the entire situation
- Ways of dealing with reluctant or recalcitrant witnesses
- Means of coordinating the investigation with legal counsel
- How to identify and review circumstantial evidence such as corporate actions, events, and documents as well as how to assess personal interviews
- How to make credibility judgments on the basis of more than simply gut feelings
- How to mediate employee disputes to structure resolutions satisfactory to all parties
- Recommendations for disciplinary levels based on the facts uncovered and the credibility judgments made
- Documentation for the situation, for both internal and external reference checks

Using Exit Interviews

Exit interviews can be valuable in assessing the overall health of an organization, as well as for identifying possible trouble spots. Since exiting employees may be willing and able to bring specific situations to the attention of a skilled and caring questioner, employers who fail to take advantage of these opportunities may be denying themselves a chance for early detection of serious problems.

Exit interview questionnaires should contain a specific reference to sexual harassment concerns. Consider asking whether the environment was ever uncomfortable because of sexually suggestive actions or materials, as well as about any incidents of touching or any links of sexual submission to offers of employment, promotions, job retention, or specific assignments.

Of course, if the questionnaire or interview raises the possibility of an unreported incident, the interviewer should try to learn as much as possible about the situation. If the interviewer is not a human resources professional trained in dealing with sexual harassment issues, the matter should be turned over to such a designated individual for immediate review and action, while the exiting employee is available for further discussion.

Should the resulting review indicate a more widespread problem, a full-scale investigation into patterns and practices should be undertaken.

If the exiting employee is leaving because of a harassment incident, either real or perceived, request that the individual remain on the job until the matter can be fully reviewed. Should the employee then leave and later level a charge of sexual harassment, claiming that she was constructively discharged, the company can argue in its defense that, in light of its commitment to review and resolve the matter promptly, a reasonable person would not have felt compelled to resign.

Should an investigation result in a finding that separation was likely caused by sexual harassment, the organization should not hesitate to explore the possibilities of reversing any personnel actions tainted by the harassment, up to and including the separation itself.

Other Proactive Opportunities

Walking the Floors

A quick and simple preventive measure with significant potential payoff is simply to tour the office premises. As you walk through, look and/or listen for:

- Any displays of a sexual nature in offices, cubicles, and other public spaces, such as posters, inappropriate magazines, and suggestive calendars.
- Any displays or graffiti in restrooms, photocopy rooms, locker rooms, or in nooks and crannies.
- Any general exchanges where the content is sexual or harassing in nature. Friday afternoons are a good time for this kind of informal check.

Discuss any concerns with the supervisor or manager involved so that preventive action can be taken in a low-key, course-of-business way.

Rumor and Innuendo

Human resources professionals and line managers are frequently in a position to hear the latest corporate gossip. While we all know that exaggeration and elaboration are the gossiper's stock in trade, we also know that there is usually a kernel of truth inside the mass of rumor and innuendo. When whispers have to do with possible sexual harassment, particularly when the same players are featured again and again, the employer ignores these rumors at its peril. Discreet inquiries may well uncover a situation that requires fast and professional intervention.

Complaint-Resolution Audits

Another good preventive measure is to conduct an informal audit of the organization's internal complaint-resolution system. Look for:

- *The level of organizational use.* This can be viewed as a percentage of the staff as a whole, or as a percentage of charge or lawsuit activity, or in any other way that makes sense in the context of the organization. If few or none of the situations that later evolved into administrative charges or civil suits were initially handled through the internal complaint-resolution system, or at least were known to appropriate line or staff people, the organization's system needs to be resuscitated. This line of inquiry should not be confined to cases of sexual harassment but applies to all employment law matters, including all of Title VII's provisions and wrongful discharge issues.

▪ *Credibility.* This is how the resolutions that the system produces are perceived by users of the system as well as by observers (all other employees). Annual employee surveys on a full range of employee concerns is a fine way to gather quantitative data on this as well as on many other useful topics. Qualitative data as a result of staff experiences and office scuttlebutt may, however, prove even more reliable on credibility issues.

▪ *Trust.* This is the extent to which users and potential users believe they will not be penalized or experience retaliation for raising their concerns through the designated channels. One of the best ways of assessing the employee trust level is through informal chats with past users of the system, looking to find out how they have been treated since lodging a complaint. Even one instance of retaliatory action can poison the view of the system for a significant time afterward.

Breathing new life into a moribund internal complaint-resolution system is a slow and difficult process, made even more so by any negative history that needs to be overcome. But nurturing the system can pay extraordinary dividends in both more positive employee relations and decreased employee litigation, with the associated decrease in time and money spent on litigation defense. Start by promoting the system in an honest and straightforward way. Then take one or two opportunities to shepherd complaints through the system, making sure that notions of fairness and nonretaliation are applied, regardless of outcome. Make sure that all levels of management, but particularly top management, understand the importance of a well-functioning internal complaint resolution system, and are willing to do what is necessary to make it happen. This in-depth monitoring may be needed for quite some time, until the credibility and trust that make the system function well have been rebuilt.

Minimizing Defamation Risks in Reference Giving

Preventive steps can help an organization minimize the defamation risks inherent in sexual harassment situations. Since harm to reputation is the essence of a defamation claim, sexual harassment investigators must always safeguard the reputations of all involved during and after the review process. Regardless of the outcome, employers will sooner or later need to respond to prospective employers, credit grantors, and others inquiring about current or former employees involved in sexual harassment situations. In addition to following the general investigative guidelines on references and defamation in Chapters 5 and 9, employers can prevent defamation or tortious claims of interference with contractual relationships by:

- Structuring the flow in inquiries. Ideally, specific individuals are designated to handle all requests for employment inquiries. These designees can be anyone with access to employee records who has been trained in the legal pitfalls of giving references. By designating one person, or a small number of responders, employers increase their chances for consistent, legally defensible replies while relieving line managers of the burden of time-consuming reference checks or the risk of personal liability.

- Requiring that all inquiries be in writing. This simple step helps ensure that only serious questioners with a real need to know pursue reference inquiries, while providing the identity of the requesting individual and organization. Whether responses are provided orally or in writing, the company will have a record of the date of request, the requesting organization, and the specific information requested as well as whether or not it was provided.

- Obtaining written releases from employees before providing third parties with reference information. This can most easily be done as part of other disclaimers, acknowledgments, and permissions usually found on applications for employment. Knowing that a written waiver was obtained when employees applied for work frees the employer to provide relevant and pertinent information in a timely and discreet way without the need to track employees or former employees down and attempt to convince them that signing a release is advantageous to them as well as to the employer.

▪ Separating fact from fiction. The employees giving references should be cautioned on the need to state reference information in an objective, factual manner, eliminating as much as humanly possible the temptation to digress into rumor, gossip, innuendo, or opinion. This is particularly true in phone situations when experienced and friendly information solicitors do everything in their power to obtain more than just facts.

▪ Developing a companywide policy on the type and extent of information to be shared and implementing it uniformly. Such a policy should be designed in consultation with competent consultants or legal counsel, who can help employers weigh the competing risks and decide on what they will divulge, based partly on legal developments in defamation issues in their own jurisdictions.

Getting References

A relatively new area of common-law negligence is the rapidly evolving one of negligent hiring or negligent retention. This new risk generally involves one of three situations:

1. An employer's failure to identify an applicant's incompetence or unfitness
2. An employer's failure to know of an employee's unfitness or the company's failure to take action based on its knowledge to correct the situation, such as transfer, retraining, or discipline
3. An employer's action providing an unfit employee with the means to harm others, such as access to private homes or apartments, access to children, or access to motor vehicles

While the majority of these cases have involved situations in which employers are hiring for janitorial or building maintenance, or for caregiver jobs, there is clear relevance to most office situations in that employers have a duty to provide a safe and harassment-free workplace. Employers hiring individuals without inquiry into such possible problems as criminal convictions for sexual assault or rape, or histories of mental illness involving violence or abuse of others, will increasingly be subject to unexpected and unwanted litigation and its attendant negative publicity.

In addition to many of the preventive measures recommended for employers giving references, these suggestions may prove useful in obtaining references:

- Carefully review the application forms of all serious contenders for a position. Look for any gaps, responses to questions on criminal convictions and bonding potential, and reasons for leaving. If gaps or inconsistencies exist, probe for more information during the interview.

- Carefully check each applicant's personal and professional references, emphasizing character issues such as honesty, trustworthiness, and reliability as well as performance matters. Attempt through follow-up and open-ended questions to obtain specific rather than general descriptions of the individual's character and abilities. Specifically inquire about workplace violence and occurrences of sexual harassment. Document all responses, whether orally or in writing, and all attempts to receive responses, even if these were not forthcoming.

- Particularly for jobs involving young people, customer contact, or use of dangerous equipment, consider using the services of a reliable and inexpensive background-checking organization. These companies have come into being in the last few years. They often have access to computerized records that employers will never be able to see, and can quickly and easily conduct anything from a routine check (which should include motor vehicle information, credit history, employment history, and any criminal record) to a complete background check involving personal interviews with neighbors, friends, and associates. A knowledgeable consultant or your legal counsel can help balance the risks with the protections and develop a reference-checking strategy that makes sense for the organization and its jobs.

Many states have restrictions on consideration of criminal records in hiring, and the Fair Credit Reporting Act requires that applicants rejected because of some types of reports be given information on the investigating organization and the facts it reported. Some employers, particularly smaller ones, may need help installing procedures to minimize these hiring risks while maximizing the protection that a full reference check can provide. The effort, however, is well worth the result when negligent hiring or retention factors may force employers to face the possibility of jury trials and punitive damage awards.

NOTES

1. 687 F. Supp 848 (SD N.Y. 1988).
2. 29 CFR §1604.11(c) (1986).

Appendix A

Sample Questions to Ask in a Sexual Harassment Investigation

Here are some suggested questions for interviews with the complainant, the accused, and other relevant parties. These sample questions illustrate the kind of inquiry that must be made and the areas that must be covered. In keeping with the information in Chapters 6 through 8, questions should be modified as to both content and language, as circumstances suggest.

For the Complainant

What exactly happened?

To the best of your recollection, using his words, what did he say to you?

Where on your body did he touch you? In what way did he touch you?

What did you say to him immediately before the incident?

Where did this occur? Was it in the workplace, and if so, specifically where?

Did this occur outside of work, or at a work-related function? Exactly where?

When did this occur? At what time of day or night?

During what workplace activity?

What was the context of the behavior? Did he treat it as a joke? How do you know he was serious?

What were you wearing? What was he wearing?

What kind of relationship had you had with him in the past? How would you describe it? How do you think he would describe it? Why is there such a difference?

Was it strictly business or did you ever go out for lunch or dinner or other forms of socializing, alone or as part of a group?

Did you meet for lunch in the building, or for coffee breaks? Did you participate in the same company-sponsored extracurricular activities?

Had you ever dated? What happened?

How long have you known each other? Who else would know of your relationship?

Have you ever given him any reason to believe you might not object to this behavior? Has he ever done anything like it to you in the past? What did you do then?

How would he know you objected to it now? What did you say or do that would have told him that? Did he seem surprised at your response?

What is the atmosphere like in this work unit? Is there a lot of joking or teasing about sexual matters? Are there any sexual materials on the walls or desks?

What form does the comraderie in the work group take and how did you feel about it? Did your manager know about this atmosphere? How would he have known? When do you think he first found out? What did he do about it?

How has the behavior affected you? Have you had a problem with your raises, opportunities for promotion or assignments, or some other aspect of work? What explanation did your supervisor give you about that? What did you do then?

Have you ever brought a similar complaint to management's attention? When was that, and what were the circumstances? What ultimately happened? How did you feel about that?

Is there a large gap between the time of the incident and the report of it? How do you account for it? What made you decide to come forward now?

Are there any possible witnesses to the incident? Who could have seen or heard something relevant?

Did you tell anyone about the incident at the time? Since? Who have you told? What is your relationship to them?

Are you aware of anyone else in the workplace who may have experienced similar behavior from the same person? Who is that and why do you believe that has occurred?

What do you want? What would you like to see happen? If it were up to you, what would the ideal solution be? Would you like to take responsibility for making any part of the solution possible? What would you feel comfortable doing?

Do you understand what will happen next and how the investigation will continue? Do you understand who will ultimately decide how this situation will be resolved? Should we look at what we can do to help you until the investigation is over, or do you feel all right about returning to your work group?

For the Accused

Do you know why I'm here?

What would you like to say in response to the brief summary I've just given you?

What do you believe happened during the incident she talks about?

What actually occurred? What did she say? What did you say?

Did you touch her? Where on her body did you touch her? What was your purpose? What did she say or do immediately before and after the touching?

Where did this occur? In a workplace location? Specifically? Or did it occur off the premises? At a business-related function? As part of a social outing? Who else was there?

When was this? At what time of the day or night?

What were you wearing? What was she wearing?

Are there any aspects to her complaint that are true? What are they? What do you disagree with? What do you not recall?

Is there anyone else who might have seen or heard something relevant to our discussion? Who are they? What would they have seen or heard?

Did you tell anyone about the incident at the time? Later? Who did you tell, and when? What is your relationship with that individual?

What kind of overall climate is there in the work group? Is there a lot of sexual joking or teasing? Did she ever join in and take part in it? When did she participate? What exactly did she do in participating?

Had her participating behavior changed recently? When did this happen? Why do you think it happened? What was the reaction of her coworkers to the change?

When did you learn about this kind of behavior in the work group? How did you learn about it? Did you participate in it? What did you do about it? Did you attempt to stop it, and if so, how?

How would you describe your relationship with her? Was it strictly business, entirely personal, or a mix?

How long have you known her? How do you think she would describe your relationship? Who else would be in a position to know its nature and be able to describe it accurately?

Had you ever behaved in a similar way with the complainant in the past? When did this happen? What did you do at that time? What was her reaction to it? What did she say to you, what did she do? Did her reaction change recently? Did she do or say anything to make you believe she had changed her mind and now felt differently? What was it that led you to think so? Why do you believe this change occurred?

What was the business or management rationale for your rating, raise, or promotion decisions about her? What kind of documentation for that exists? Where is it and what does it consist of? If usual policies and practices were not followed in her case, why not?

Why would she be saying these terrible things about you? What would motivate her to bring a claim that wasn't true?

What are you prepared to do about the situation? How would you suggest resolving it?

Do you understand how this investigation will continue and who will ultimately decide how the situation will be resolved? Do you understand that no one in the organization is permitted to retaliate against this employee for bringing this allegation to our attention, and that the consequences for doing so are substantial?

For Relevant Others

Have you ever personally seen or heard anything to indicate that she was being made uncomfortable at work, or that she found her work environment offensive? What did you see or hear? Who was making things uncomfortable? In what way?

Did complainant ever tell you about this incident? What did she tell you? When was that?

What kind of relationship would you say she had with him? Was it strictly business, entirely personal, or a mix? How long have they known each other? What would you say was going on with them?

What kind of relationship did she have with the supervisor? Was he aware of the problem? How do you know? What did he do about it? What details can you provide of that? Do you know when it happened, what time, where?

What exactly did you see or hear? What happened then?

Who else might know something about this?

Do you understand the need to discuss this with no one else, at work or outside of work? Do you agree to do that?

How do you feel about the situation? What kind of relationship do you have with her, with him, with the supervisor?

Appendix B

Glossary of Legal Terms

Agency   The relationship in which one individual (the agent) acts for or on the behalf of or represents another (the principal) by the authority granted to the actor by the principal.

Common Law Negligence Claims   Negligence actions based on English common law, the foundation of the American legal system. Negligence is the failure to do what a reasonably careful person would under the same circumstances, or to do what a reasonable person in similar circumstances would not.

Compelled Self-Publication   Defamation doctrine that holds employers using neutral reference policies liable for former employees' communication of their terminations when the facts underlying the terminations are questionable.

Compensatory Damages   The amount of money awarded to individuals to make them whole or place them in the position they would have been in had the situation they complained of never occurred; actual losses.

Constructive Discharge   The theory that a resignation from employment may actually be treated as a dismissal, since the employer's imposition of intolerable terms and conditions of employment gave the resigning employee no choice but to leave.

Defamation   Damage to a person's reputation or good name through publication of a falsehood to a third party.

Disparate Impact   Discriminatory effect that results unintentionally from use of an instrument—for example, a preemployment test—that is neutral on its face.

Hostile Environment   One of the two types of sexual harassment claims; requires showing of frequent, nontrivial acts of a sexual nature that create the effect of a hostile, offensive, or intimidating working atmosphere. No money damages are required to be shown.

Injunctive Relief   An equitable remedy ordered by the court requiring that certain activities stop, such as that an organization refrain from discrimination against women in the future.

Negligent Hiring   Tort action against employers who fail to protect employees from foreseeable harm by carefully checking references of new employees.

Negligent Referral   A potential tort action by a hiring employer against an original employer who fails to disclose information that would have prevented a foreseeable risk to others.

Negligent Retention   Tort action against employers who fail to remove individuals before they cause foreseeable harm to others.

Neutral Reference Policy   Approach of many employers who restrict reference information disclosed to others to objective, basic facts only.

Paramour Preference   The term used to refer to the natural preference of a decision maker for the individual with whom he or she has an ongoing social or sexual relationship over others in the workplace.

Punitive Damages   The money amount awarded by juries or specified by statute to individuals so that the defendant is punished for his or her conduct and all potential defendants will be effectively deterred from so acting.

Quid Pro Quo   One of the two types of sexual harassment claims; requires showing of unwelcome activity of a sexual nature in exchange for tangible job benefit, or the loss of tangible job benefit owing to the rejection of such activity. Fundamentally, an abuse of supervisory power.

Reasonable Person/Woman   The mythical judicial construct of an individual who thinks and responds the way an ordinary, logical, and careful person/woman would under the same conditions; a standard for behavior.

Respondeat Superior   Literally, "let the master answer," the principle that the master is responsible for the acts of the servant.

Sex Discrimination   The cause of action recognized by Title VII and many state statutes; the favoring of one individual or group over another on the basis of gender or stereotypical assumptions associated with gender.

Sexual Harassment   A cause of action grounded in sex discrimination; the imposition of unwelcome sexual conduct on an employee in the workplace.

Strict Liability   The automatic imposition of liability, regardless of extenuating circumstances or intent.

Tort   A civil wrong, redressed by money damages.

Unwelcome Conduct   Behavior that is considered offensive to and undesirable by its recipient; behavior that is not encouraged or incited by its recipient.

Index